Soul Ties

Discerning and Redeeming Ungodly

Soul Ties

Discerning and Redeeming Ungodly

Vinu V Das

Tabor Press

ISBN 978-1-997541-14-1

Table of Contents

Chapter 1 – Introducing Soul Ties..............................13

1.1 Definition & Scope 13

    1.1.1 Etymology of "soul" and "tie" 14

    1.1.2 Modern Usage vs. Biblical Nuance 15

1.2 Biblical Snapshots of Strong Bonds 16

    1.2.1 David & Jonathan (1 Samuel 18)...............17

    1.2.2 Jacob & Benjamin (Genesis 44) 18

1.3 Purpose of This Book 19

    1.3.1 Spiritual discernment 19

    1.3.2 Pathways to freedom 20

Chapter 2 – Foundations in Scripture & Theology 22

2.1 Soul, Spirit, and Body: A Quick Theology 22

    2.1.1 Trichotomy vs. Dichotomy Debate 23

2.2 Covenant Language in the Old Testament 24

    2.2.1 "Cleaving" and "Knitting" Verbs 24

2.3 New-Covenant Insights...............26

    2.3.1 Unity with Christ (1 Corinthians 6:17) 26

    2.3.2 The Body of Christ & Interpersonal Bonds 27

Chapter 3 – Categories of Soul Ties 29

3.1 Godly Soul Ties...............29

    3.1.1 Marriage Covenants 29

    3.1.2 Spiritual Mentorship & Discipleship 30

    3.1.3 Christian Fellowship & Accountability 31

3.1.4 Family Covenantal Ties 31

3.2 Ungodly Soul Ties 32

3.2.1 Sexual & Marital Betrayal 32

3.2.2 Codependent & Toxic Friendships 32

3.2.3 Occultic & Idolatrous Bonds 33

3.2.4 Emotional Abuse & Manipulative Relationships 33

3.3 Neutral or Seasonal Soul Ties 33

3.3.1 Family Transitions & Launching Children 34

3.3.2 Workplace & Ministry Partnerships 34

3.3.3 Community & Cultural Connections 34

3.3.4 Digital & Social-Media Ties 34

3.4 Discerning the Category of a Soul Tie 35

Chapter 4 – How Soul Ties Are Formed 36

4.1 Physical Unity 36

4.1.1 Sexual Intimacy 37

4.1.2 Shared Bodily Trauma 38

4.2 Emotional & Psychological Doors 39

4.2.1 Empathy Gone Unhealthy 40

4.3 Spiritual & Covenantal Doors 41

4.3.1 Oaths, Vows, and Rituals 41

4.4 Additional Pathways to Formation 42

4.4.1 Shared Mission & Sacrifice 43

4.4.2 Fear & Control as Bonding Agents 43

Chapter 5 – Discernment: Signs & Symptoms 44

5.1 Behavioral Indicators 44

5.1.1 Compulsive Preoccupation 45

5.1.2 Impaired Boundaries 45

5.1.3 Pattern of Repetitive Choices 46

5.1.4 Withdrawal from Community 46

5.2 Emotional Indicators 47

5.2.1 Unexplained Guilt or Shame 47

5.2.2 Persistent Longing or Nostalgia 48

5.2.3 Anxiety and Fear Patterns 48

5.2.4 Enmeshment and Loss of Self 49

5.3 Spiritual Indicators 49

5.3.1 Hindrance in Prayer Life 49

5.3.2 Spiritual Dryness and Despair 50

5.3.3 Disruption of Vision and Direction 50

5.3.4 Recurring Sin Patterns 51

Chapter 6 – Consequences of Ungodly Soul Ties 52

6.1 Distorted Identity 52

6.1.1 Erosion of Self-Worth 53

6.1.2 Confused Identity in Christ 53

6.1.3 Identity Masking and Performance 54

6.2 Repetitive Sin Cycles 54

6.2.1 Bondage to Patterns of Sin 54

6.2.2 Legalistic Religion and False Guilt 55

6.2.3 Spiritual Oppression and Temptation Amplification 55

6.3 Relational Sabotage 56

6.3.1 Breakdown of Trust 56

6.3.2 Isolation from Healthy Community 56

6.3.3 Impairment of Ministry and Calling 57

Chapter 7 – Breaking Unhealthy Soul Ties 58

7.1 Repentance & Renunciation 58

7.1.1 Confession and Repentance 59

7.1.2 Renunciation Prayers 59

7.1.3 Breaking Generational Curses 61

7.1.4 Forgiveness of Others and Self 61

7.2 Deliverance & Inner-Healing Models 62

7.2.1 Exercising Authority in Christ 62

7.2.2 Prayer Models for Deliverance 63

7.2.3 Inner-Healing: Heart-Level Repair 64

7.2.4 Role of the Holy Spirit in Healing 64

7.2.5 Professional Help: Pastoral Counseling & Therapy 65

7.3 Establishing Boundaries 65

7.3.1 Scriptural Basis for Boundaries 65

7.3.2 Types of Boundaries 65

7.3.3 Practical Steps to Set Boundaries 66

7.3.4 Maintaining Boundaries and Accountability 66

7.3.5 Loving but Wise Boundaries 67

Chapter 8 – Healing & Restoration After Severance 68

8.1 Grieving the Loss of a Bond 68

8.1.1 Recognizing the Need to Grieve 69

8.1.2 Stages of Grief in a Spiritual Context 69

8.1.3 Rituals and Practices to Process Loss 70

8.2 Rebuilding Self-Worth in Christ 70

8.2.1 Understanding Your New Identity 70

8.2.2 Renewing the Mind through Scripture 71

8.2.3 Practicing Self-Compassion and Spiritual Self-Care 71

8.3 Community & Accountability 72

8.3.1 Communing with the Body of Christ.............72

8.3.2 Finding Safe Relationships for Accountability 73

8.3.3 Professional and Pastoral Support 73

8.4 Walking Forward in Newness 73

Chapter 9 – Building Godly Relationships Going Forward...........75

9.1 Biblical Friendship Ethics 75

9.1.1 Choosing Friends Wisely................................76

9.1.2 Qualities of a Godly Friend 76

9.1.3 Cultivating Mutual Encouragement...............77

9.1.4 Conflict Resolution and Forgiveness..............78

9.2 Courtship & Dating with Discernment 79

9.2.1 Defining Biblical Courtship............................79

9.2.2 Setting Boundaries in Dating 80

9.2.3 Evaluating Character and Spiritual Alignment..............81

9.2.4 Intentional Community Involvement 81

9.3 Marriage: Keeping the Bond Holy 82

9.3.1 Covenantal Foundations...............................82

9.3.2 Cultivating Spiritual Intimacy.. 83

9.3.3 Seasonal Support and Conflict Management 83

9.3.4 Nurturing Family Worship and Legacy..........84

Chapter 10 – Special Contexts & Contemporary Challenges 85

10.1 Family Systems & Generational Ties 85

10.1.1 Multigenerational Patterns 86

10.1.2 Birth Order, Roles, and Expectations..........................86

10.1.3 Breaking Generational Soul Ties..............................87

10.1.4 Recasting Family Identity in Christ...........................87

10.2 Digital-Age Soul Ties 87

10.2.1 Virtual Relationships & Emotional Bonding...............88

10.2.2 Social Media & Comparative Idolatry 88

10.2.3 Online Intimacy & Pornography 89

10.2.4 Digital Fast & Media Boundaries 90

10.3 Ministry & Leadership Pitfalls 91

10.3.1 Codependent Pastoral Bonds 91

10.3.2 Celebrity Christian Culture 92

10.3.3 Power Dynamics & Spiritual Abuse 92

10.3.4 Healthy Leader-Congregant Soul Ties....................93

Chapter 11 – Case Studies & Testimonies 94

11.1 Personal Narratives of Freedom 94

11.1.1 Sarah's Journey from Codependency to
Christ-Centered Identity 94

11.1.2 Mark's Breakthrough from Pornography Soul Tie 96

11.1.3 Maria's Liberation from Generational Patterns..........97

11.2 Pastoral Counseling Vignettes 98

11.2.1 The Thompsons' Marriage Restoration 98

11.2.2 Deliverance Session with "Mark & Lisa"................99

11.2.3 Small-Group Intervention in Workplace Addiction ..100

11.3 Analytical Commentary on Each Story 101

11.3.1 Patterns Observed 101

11.3.2 Common Barriers to Freedom 102

11.3.3 Keys to Sustainable Redemption 102

Chapter 12 – Tools, Prayers & Further Resources 103

12.1 Guided Prayer Templates 103

12.1.1 Prayer for Discernment 104

12.1.2 Prayer for Breaking Soul Ties........................104

12.1.3 Prayer for Healing Wounds 105

12.1.4 Prayer for Cultivating New Godly Bonds 105

12.2 Journaling Prompts for Self-Examination 106

12.2.1 Identifying Hidden Ties...............................106

12.2.2 Mapping Emotional Triggers 106

12.2.3 Recording Deliverance Progress 107

12.2.4 Celebrations of Freedom 107

12.3 Recommended Reading & Ministries............................108

12.3.1 Classic Theological Works...........................108

12.3.2 Contemporary Books on Boundaries, Deliverance, and Healing...108

12.3.3 Reputable Ministries and Online Resources.............109

12.3.4 Counseling and Retreat Centers 109

12.4 Small-Group Discussion Guide 110

12.4.1 Week 1: Understanding Soul Ties...........................110

12.4.2 Week 2: Identifying Personal Ties 111

12.4.3 Week 3: Prayer and Deliverance 111

12.4.4 Week 4: Healing and Restoration 111

12.4.5 Week 5: Building Godly Relationships 112

12.4.6 Facilitator's Tips and Confidentiality Guidelines 112

Chapter 1 – Introducing Soul Ties

The phenomenon commonly referred to as "soul ties" has captured the attention of pastors, counselors, and lay believers alike. While the term itself is not found in the biblical text, it describes the deep connections—spiritual, emotional, and sometimes physical—that bind individuals together. These bonds can reflect God-honoring relationships marked by covenant love, or unhealthy attachments that hinder spiritual growth. In this chapter, we will define what we mean by soul ties, explore their linguistic roots and modern connotations, examine two foundational biblical examples, and sketch the goals of this work: to sharpen your spiritual discernment and to chart a clear path toward wholeness and freedom.

1.1 Definition & Scope

The phrase "soul tie" brings to mind an invisible cord that links two souls. But what exactly is being tied, and how broad is the scope of such connections?

At its core, a soul tie refers to a bond so strong that the inner life of one person becomes intertwined with that of another.

These bonds may arise through various forms of unity—physical intimacy, shared suffering, deep friendship, or solemn vows. Just as Christ speaks of the vine and branches (John 15:5), so too human hearts can become joined in ways that profoundly impact thoughts, emotions, and behavior.

Yet not every tight relationship qualifies as a soul tie in our discussion. We reserve the term for connections that create a lasting, often unconscious, influence over one's affections or allegiances. In healthy marriage or mentorship, such ties are rooted in Christ-centered covenant and bear good fruit. In contrast, ties formed through sexual immorality, manipulative friendships, or spiritual pacts can introduce confusion, guilt, and spiritual oppression (1 Cor 6:16–17).

Within this book, we will explore both sides of the ledger: **godly soul ties**, which reflect Christ's own covenantal love, and **ungodly soul ties**, which fracture our identity and hinder fellowship with God. Our starting point is a clear definition—one that distinguishes between the psychological influence of close bonds and the deeper, spiritual ramifications of soul ties.

1.1.1 Etymology of "soul" and "tie"

To appreciate the depth of soul ties, we must first consider the meaning of the words "soul" and "tie" in their original languages.

Soul. In the Old Testament, the Hebrew word most often translated "soul" is נֶפֶשׁ (nephesh), which denotes the life-breath, the seat of emotions, desires, and personal identity. Genesis 2:7 declares, "then the LORD God formed the man of dust from the ground and breathed into his nostrils the breath of life, and the man became a living **nephesh**." In the New Testament, the Greek equivalent is ψυχή (psuchē), similarly signifying the inner life or self (Matthew 10:28; Mark 8:36). Thus when we speak of the "soul," we are referring not to an immaterial entity detached from the body, but the very essence of personhood—will, emotion, and vitality combined.

Tie. The notion of a bond or tie is conveyed in several Hebrew and Greek terms. In Hebrew, the verb דָּ בַ ק (*dabaq*) means "to cling" or "stick" (Genesis 2:24: "a man shall leave his father and mother and **dabaq** to his wife"), while חָ בַ ק (*chabaq*) carries a sense of embracing or binding together (e.g., Psalm 139:13: "For you formed my **inward parts**; you **knit** me together in my mother's womb"). The Greek New Testament speaks of συνδέω (*syndeō*), "to bind together," and κοινωνία (*koinōnia*), "sharing" or "fellowship," which implies a mutual participation in life.

When combined, the composite idea is of two persons "clinging" to the very core of each other's being—emotions, conscience, and spiritual vitality bound inextricably. It is crucial to note, however, that while covenants of Scripture employ these terms for marriage, community, and God's own relationship with His people, the specific term "soul tie" is a modern construct. Our task is to view it through the lens of biblical language, grounding the concept in the rich soil of Scripture rather than mere psychological parlance.

1.1.2 Modern Usage vs. Biblical Nuance

In recent decades, Christian counselors and authors have popularized "soul ties" as a framework for understanding why certain relationships feel so unbreakable. Authors such as Dr. Frank Minirth and Dr. Paul Meier introduced the idea in the late twentieth century, elaborating categories—spiritual soul ties, sexual soul ties, soul ties by wrong vows, and so forth. Their aim was pastoral: to give believers a language for the guilt, compulsions, or spiritual hindrances they experienced after certain relationships.

Modern pastoral context. Today, many churches offer "soul tie" seminars, teaching that sexual sin creates a spiritual cord linking partners; that covenants in pagan rituals can form soul ties; and that deep friendships sometimes require deliverance ministry to sever unhealthy bonds. These teachings typically include prayer protocols, renunciation of vows, and sometimes visual exercises (e.g., cutting cords in prayer). Such approaches have ministered deliverance and clarity to many, yet they can also be misapplied, leading to spiritual anxiety or overspiritualizing normal grief at relational loss.

Biblical nuance. The Bible never issues a blanket injunction to renounce vague soul ties; rather, it addresses specific covenant breaches and patterns of sin. For example, sexual immorality is condemned because it unites believers to a "prostitute," making them one body with her (1 Cor 6:16). False covenants or occult vows are denounced (Deut 23:18; Acts 19:18–19) because they carry spiritual consequences. But the biblical solution is not a generic "cut the cord" ceremony; it is **repentance, forgiveness**, and **restoration** through Christ's atoning work (1 John 1:9).

Moreover, many modern definitions blur the line between **spiritual oppression** and **psychological attachment**. Attachment theory in secular psychology describes how early bonds shape adult relationships, but it does not invoke demons or unclean spirits. The biblical picture is broader: the soul tie concept must account for spiritual reality—Christ's indwelling Spirit, demonic influences, and the believer's union with Christ—alongside emotional and psychological factors.

In this book, we will preserve the pastoral insights of the modern "soul tie" movement—especially its emphasis on recognizing unhealthy bonds—while re-anchoring the practice in biblical theology. We will discern between what the Bible attributes to sin's spiritual power (e.g., addiction to a person, demonic strongholds) and what belongs to natural human grief or dependence. This balanced approach prevents both reductionist psychology and unchecked spiritualization, offering a holistic path to freedom.

1.2 Biblical Snapshots of Strong Bonds

To ground our discussion in Scripture, we turn to two vivid narratives where deep bonds shape destiny and demonstrate both the beauty and risks of soul-level connections. While not exhaustive, these examples illustrate how the Bible depicts covenant-like ties and hint at the dynamics we later label "soul ties."

1.2.1 David & Jonathan (1 Samuel 18)

The friendship of David and Jonathan stands as perhaps the quintessential biblical portrait of a godly soul tie. In 1 Samuel 18:1–4, we read:

> "As soon as he had finished speaking to Saul, the soul of Jonathan was knit to the soul of David, and Jonathan loved him as his own soul. And Saul took him that day and would not let him return to his father's house. Then Jonathan made a covenant with David, because he loved him as his own soul. And Jonathan stripped himself of the robe that was on him and gave it to David, and his armor, and even his sword and his bow and his belt." (ESV)

Several elements stand out:

- **Mutual affection "as his own soul."** The Hebrew phrase בְנַפְשׁוֹ נֶפֶשׁ קָחֲבַ (*chaveq nephesh benafsho*) conveys a love so deep it mirrors self-love. Jonathan's willingness to forsake royal privileges and share his identity with David testifies to a bond that transcends familial or political allegiance.
- **Covenantal act.** Jonathan and David formalize their bond through a covenant, a solemn agreement involving symbolic exchange (robes, weapons). Covenants in Scripture often ratify enduring relationships—God's covenant with Israel (Exodus 24), marriage covenants (Malachi 2:14), and dynastic covenants (2 Samuel 7).
- **Longevity and sacrifice.** This bond endures through years of exile, danger, and—even after Jonathan's death—David's grief (2 Samuel 1:26: "Your love to me was wonderful, passing the love of women"). True soul ties, when rooted in godly covenant, call for sacrificial loyalty and prompt poetry of lament.

Jonathan's example provides a benchmark for holy friendship: a union that delights in another's flourishing, expresses itself in heartfelt commitment, and ultimately honors God. It also reminds us that such bonds, though beautiful, carry weight: they shape identity, direct loyalties, and call for perseverance under trial.

1.2.2 Jacob & Benjamin (Genesis 44)

In a different register, the story of Jacob (Israel) and his youngest son Benjamin offers another snapshot of a soul-level bond—this time colored by parental love and the risk of relational anguish. During Joseph's hidden test in Egypt (Genesis 44:1–34), Judah pleads with the Egyptian ruler:

> "Now then, please let your servant remain as a slave to my lord instead of the boy, and let the boy go back with his brothers. For how can I go back to my father if the boy is not with me?… For your servant became surety for the boy to my father, saying, 'If I do not bring him back to you, then I will bear the blame before my father all my life.'" (Gen 44:33–34, ESV)

Key points:

- **"Bound up in the lad's life."** The Hebrew verb used—חָבַק (chabaq)—denotes an embrace or binding together. Judah's life is entwined with Benjamin's fate. Such language echoes the intimate "knitting" language of Psalm 139:13 and points to a bond that transcends mere affection—it is existential.
- **Parental covenant.** Unlike Jonathan's voluntary covenant with David, here we see a familial tie sealed through parental oath. Jacob had previously vowed, "If pain kills me, I have earned it" in Jacob's wrestling narrative (Gen 32:26–27), indicating the seriousness with which vows were made and the spiritual weight they carried.

- **Emotional urgency.** The intensity of Judah's plea captures the agony that arises when a soul tie is threatened. Even amid famine, political intrigue, and half-brother rivalry, Judah prioritizes Benjamin above his own safety, demonstrating how soul ties shape decisions and moral priorities.

The Jacob–Benjamin example reminds us that soul ties extend beyond friendship or sexual union; family relationships can create equally powerful bonds—ones that bring profound joy but also the risk of despair when broken or manipulated.

1.3 Purpose of This Book

Having set the stage linguistically and biblically, we clarify why this book is both timely and essential for every believer navigating relationships in a complex world.

1.3.1 Spiritual discernment

First, we aim to **sharpen your spiritual discernment** regarding the ties that bind. In an age where therapy jargon often crowds out spiritual categories, Christians need to distinguish between legitimate emotional attachments, unhealthy psychological patterns, and true spiritual entanglements. Hebrews 5:14 exhorts us: "But solid food is for the mature, for those who have their powers of discernment trained by constant practice to distinguish good from evil."

- **Good vs. mixed vs. evil ties.** We will learn to recognize the hallmarks of godly soul ties—covenantal promises kept in love—and contrast them with mixed ties that carry both blessing and bondage, and outright ungodly ties that contravene God's design.
- **Spiritual roots of relational struggles.** Not all relationship pain is demonic, yet Ephesians 0.12 reminds us that "we do not wrestle against flesh and blood but against... spiritual forces of evil." Discerning when a relationship struggle is purely psychological,

when it involves spiritual strongholds, or when it is simply growth-related grief, is a key skill.

- **Biblical benchmarks.** Drawing from Scripture's own relational narratives—covenants, curses, redemptive reconciliations—we establish benchmarks for healthy communion and red flags for damaging entanglement.

By cultivating this discernment, you will be equipped to approach every relationship through a Christ-centered lens, neither ignorant of spiritual realities nor oblivious to genuine emotional dynamics.

1.3.2 Pathways to freedom

Second, this book lays out **pathways to freedom** for anyone caught in the grip of an unhealthy soul tie. True freedom in Christ encompasses repentance, renewal of mind, inner healing, and practical boundary-setting.

- **Repentance and renunciation.** Following biblical models (e.g., Peter's repentance in Galatians 2:11–14), we learn how to confess misplaced loyalties, renounce ungodly vows, and restore broken covenants through Christ's atoning blood.
- **Inner-healing and deliverance.** While not every tie requires a deliverance session, many believers find relief through focused prayer that invites the Holy Spirit to heal emotional wounds and break spiritual cords (Psalm 147:3; Luke 4:18). We will survey safe, biblically anchored practices.
- **Boundary craftsmanship.** The New Testament models for boundary-making—where Paul refuses to be spiritually yoked to an unbeliever (2 Cor 6:14–18), or Jesus slips away to solitary prayer—guide us in crafting healthy limitations on relationships that threaten our walk with God.
- **Restorative community.** Freedom is seldom achieved in isolation. James 5:16 encourages, "Therefore, confess your sins to one another and pray for one another, that you may be healed." We will

explore how small groups, pastoral care, and accountability partners play vital roles.

Ultimately, the goal is not merely severance but **redemption**—transforming even difficult bonds into opportunities for grace. As 2 Corinthians 5:18–19 reminds us, God has entrusted us with the ministry of reconciliation. Even a broken soul tie, when healed, can become a testimony of God's power to restore and unite.

Chapter 2 – Foundations in Scripture & Theology

Understanding soul ties demands a firm theological and biblical grounding. In this chapter, we'll explore how Scripture portrays the composition of human beings (soul, spirit, body), trace the language of covenantal "binding" in the Old Testament, and survey New-Covenant teachings on our union with Christ. These foundations will equip us to discern when a bond honors God's design and when it distorts it.

2.1 Soul, Spirit, and Body: A Quick Theology

At the heart of "soul ties" lies the biblical anthropology of **what we are**. The Old and New Testaments present varying—but complementary—ways of speaking about human nature: sometimes as a tripartite being (body, soul, spirit), sometimes as a bipartite being (body + immaterial). This section clarifies those categories so we can see where "soul ties" attach.

1. **The Trichotomous View**
   o **Scriptural Basis.**
     - *Body (σῶμα)*: Our material frame. "For as a man dies, so shall he live: … shall God call his own soul (נֶפֶשׁ) from the hand of the grave, even his body (גּוּף) that is laid in corruption" (Isaiah 26:19).
     - *Soul (נֶפֶשׁ/ψυχή)*: Often rendered "self," "life," or "desire." Genesis 2:7 says God formed man's *nephesh* by breathing into dust. In the New Testament, Jesus warns: "Whoever finds his life (ψυχή) will lose it…" (Matt 10:39).
     - *Spirit (רוּחַ/πνεῦμα)*: The inner breath or wind of life. Paul prays that believers be "sanctified wholly, and may your whole spirit and soul and body be preserved blameless…" (1 Thess 5:23).
   o **Theological Implications.**
     - **Spirit** is our God-ward capacity: where we commune with the Spirit of God (Rom 8:16).
     - **Soul** is our self-consciousness: will, emotions, intellect (Matt 22:37).
     - **Body** is our instrument in the world.
2. **The Dichotomous View**
   o **Scriptural Basis.**
     - Many passages refer simply to a "body" and a unified immaterial "soul" or "spirit." Hebrews 4:12 speaks of the Word dividing "soul and spirit," yet the term may signal the sharpness of God's Word rather than two distinct faculties.
     - Jesus' encounter in Mark 12:30—"You shall love the Lord your God with all your heart and with all your soul and with all your mind and with all your

strength"—lists four terms that overlap considerably, suggesting a unitary immaterial self.
- o **Theological Implications.**
  - Emphasizes **holism**: body and immaterial life constitute a single human essence made in God's image (Gen 1:27).
  - Draws attention to our **whole-person** relationship with God, rather than compartmentalized faculties.
3. **Soul Ties in Light of Both Views**
   - o Whether you favor trichotomy or dichotomy, the **imprint** of another onto our immaterial life matters. If the immaterial self is a single reality, a "soul tie" still denotes a binding in that unified self. If one distinguishes soul and spirit, ties may attach more heavily to our soul (emotional/intellectual self) but can also veer into the spirit (our God-ward communion).

2.2 Covenant Language in the Old Testament

To grasp the **binding** aspect of soul ties, we must look to the covenant vocabulary of Israel's Scriptures. Covenants in the ancient Near East often involved ceremonies, oaths, and shared symbols establishing mutual obligations. Israelic covenant language employs vivid verbs for "clinging" and "knitting" that prefigure the "binding of souls."

2.2.1 "Cleaving" and "Knitting" Verbs

1. **דָּבַק (dābaq) – "to cling, cleave."**
   - o **Genesis 2:24:** "Therefore a man shall leave his father and his mother and *cling* (*dābaq*) to his wife, and they shall become one flesh." Here, *dābaq* describes both physical and covenantal union in marriage.
   - o **Ruth 1:14:** "Then they lifted up their voices and wept again. And Orpah kissed her

mother-in-law, but Ruth *clung* (*dābaq*) to her."
Ruth's emotional covenant to Naomi transcends mere family ties, illustrating how *dābaq* binds hearts.

2. קָשַׁ ר (**qāšar**) – **"to tie, bind."**
   o **Joshua 23:8:** "But you are to hold fast (*qāšar*) to the LORD your God as you have done to this day." Here, the verb bridges covenant commitment and steadfast devotion.
   o **Psalm 62:8:** "Trust in him at all times, O people; pour out your heart before him; God is a refuge for us. Selah." While *qāšar* is not explicit, the concept of "holding" or "pouring out" correlates with binding one's self in trust.

3. תָּפַ ר (**tāpar**) / רָקַ ם (**rāqam**) – **"to weave, knit."**
   o **Psalm 139:13–14:** "For you formed my inward parts; you *knit* (*rāqam*) me together in my mother's womb. I praise you, for I am fearfully and wonderfully made." Although this is not covenantal, the imagery of intimate weaving underscores the Creator's own soul-binding craftsmanship.
   o **Exodus 39:32:** "Thus all the work of the tabernacle... was finished. And the sons of Israel did all the work, just as the Lord had commanded Moses." The meticulous "weaving" of the tabernacle fabrics points to covenant structures woven between God and His people.

4. **Covenant Objects & Actions**
   o **Shared Meals (Leviticus 7:13–15):** Eating together sealed fellowship.
   o **Blood Oaths (Exodus 24:8):** Moses sprinkled blood, signifying life-bonding agreement.
   o **Sign-Objects (Genesis 17:11):** Circumcision as a perpetual mark of the Abrahamic covenant.

Theological Insight: The same verbs and rituals that bound Israel to Yahweh under the Old Covenant, and spouses to one another, also serve as prototypes to help us understand *how* human hearts can become "knit" or "cleave" to one another—sometimes in ways the Lord intended, sometimes not.

2.3 New-Covenant Insights

While the Old Testament lays the **vocabulary** of binding, the New Covenant reconfigures the **direction** of soul ties: away from human-only covenants and into union with Christ, who fulfills and transcends all earthly bonds.

2.3.1 Unity with Christ (1 Corinthians 6:17)

1. **Scripture on Union**
   o **1 Corinthians 6:16–17:** Paul warns, "He who joins himself to a prostitute becomes one body (σῶμα) with her... But he who is joined (κολλάω) to the Lord becomes one spirit." The same verb (kollaō, "to glue or join") describes an illicit tie and a holy union, underscoring that every soul tie carries spiritual weight.
   o **John 15:4–5:** "Abide in me, and I in you... for without me you can do nothing." Christ's vine-and-branches imagery conveys an ongoing, living bond that bears fruit when maintained.
   o **Romans 6:5:** "For if we have been united (συνεσταυρωμένοι) with him in a death like his, we shall certainly be united with him in a resurrection like his." Baptism physically signs this spiritual co-death and co-resurrection.
2. **Christ as the Superior Covenant-Partner**
   o **Ephesians 5:30–32:** "'For we are members of his body...'" Paul applies the marriage covenant's language (Gen 2:24) to Christ and the Church, painting a picture of the ultimate soul tie.
   o **Hebrews 9:14–15:** Christ's blood inaugurates a "new covenant," cleansing our consciences and binding us into God's family far more deeply than any human agreement.

3. **Implications for Human Soul Ties**
    o **Priority of the Christ-Tie.** All other attachments must be secondary to our union with Christ (Matt 10:37–39).
    o **Measure of All Ties.** Any bond that draws us away from Christ's union—hinders our prayer, compromises our witness, or entangles us in sin—must be examined against the standard of our primary soul tie to Him.
    o **Healing in Christ.** Where an ungodly tie has left us wounded or enslaved, the New Covenant offers restoration: "There is therefore now no condemnation for those who are in Christ Jesus" (Rom 8:1).

2.3.2 The Body of Christ & Interpersonal Bonds

Though the outline named only 2.3.1, expanding here to cover how the **church-body language** shapes our understanding of soul ties in community.

1. **One Body, Many Members (1 Cor 12:12–27)**
    o **Unity in Diversity.** Every believer is "baptized by one Spirit into one body" (v. 13) yet given differing gifts. Soul ties within the body— mentorship, friendship, accountability—reflect and reinforce our unity.
    o **Mutual Dependence.** Paul's imagery of the foot or hand grieving if the other suffers (v. 26) shows that healthy soul ties within the church bring shared joy and sorrow.
2. **Building Up in Love (Eph 4:1–16)**
    o **Growth Through Ties.** Leaders and members, connected by soul-ties of teaching, prayer, and fellowship, enable the "whole body" to grow and mature "into the measure of the stature of the fullness of Christ" (v. 13).
    o **Warning Against Disruption.** Ungodly soul ties—gossip networks, cliques, rivalries— fracture the body and "create obstacles" to unity (v. 3).

3. **Marriage as a Gospel Witness (Eph 5:21–33)**
    o **Christ and the Church.** Husbands "ought to love their wives as their own bodies" (v. 28), illustrating the gospel. A godly marriage soul tie signifies something far greater than mutual affection: it portrays Christ's self-giving love.

Chapter 3 – Categories of Soul Ties

Not all soul ties are the same. Some reflect God's good design, building us up in Christ; others wound, ensnare, and draw us away from Him; and yet others occupy a gray zone—necessary for a season but requiring careful boundaries. In this chapter, we'll map the landscape of soul ties into three broad categories—**Godly**, **Ungodly**, and **Neutral/Seasonal**—exploring their distinct characteristics, biblical examples, and spiritual dynamics.

3.1 Godly Soul Ties

God delights in bonding believers together in ways that reflect His own triune relationship. These ties forge unity, accountability, and mutual growth as we pursue Christ together.

3.1.1 Marriage Covenants

- **One Flesh Union.** From the first marriage, God ordained a unique soul tie between husband and wife: "Therefore a man shall leave his father and his mother and hold fast to his wife, and they shall become one flesh" (Gen 2:24). That "holding fast" (*dābaq*) speaks not merely of physical union but of two entire lives—emotional, spiritual, and practical—knitting together.

- **Christ & the Church.** Paul sees marriage as a living parable of Christ's bond with His Bride: "Husbands, love your wives, as Christ loved the church and gave himself up for her… 'Therefore a man shall leave his father and mother and hold fast to his wife, and the two shall become one flesh.' This mystery is profound, and I am saying that it refers to Christ and the church" (Eph 5:25–27, 31–32). In healthy marriages, husband and wife spur one another toward holiness—mirroring the cross-shaped love of Christ.
- **Mutual Sanctification.** A godly marriage tie carries the weight of covenant faithfulness: bearing one another's sins (Gal 6:2), sharpening one another's character (Prov 27:17), and stewarding intimacy for God's glory.

3.1.2 Spiritual Mentorship & Discipleship

- **Paul & Timothy.** The apostle's "soul tie" with Timothy blends paternal affection and doctrinal transmission: "For this reason I remind you to fan into flame the gift of God… and to entrust to reliable people what you heard from me, in the presence of many witnesses" (2 Tim 1:6–7; 2:2). This tie involves both teaching and personal investment in Timothy's character.
- **Moses & Joshua.** Under Sinai's shadow, Joshua clings to Moses: "Moses summoned Joshua and said… 'Be strong and courageous, for you shall bring the people of Israel into the land that I swore to give them'" (Deut 31:7). Moses shapes Joshua's leadership through close communion and intercession.
- **Elijah & Elisha.** When Elijah throws his cloak over Elisha, he imparts prophetic authority—and his spiritual mantle: "When they crossed, Elijah said to Elisha, 'Ask what I shall do for you, before I am taken from you.' And Elisha said, 'Please let me inherit a double portion of your spirit'" (2 Kings 2:9). This bond evidences covenantal promise plus impartation.

- **Key Dynamics.** Godly mentorship soul ties:
  1. **Mutual Accountability.** Mentor prays for mentee; mentee honors mentor (1 Cor 11:1).
  2. **Doctrinal Fidelity.** The tie preserves apostolic truth (Titus 1:9).
  3. **Fruit-bearing.** Disciple-making multiplies the gospel legacy (Matt 28:19–20).

3.1.3 Christian Fellowship & Accountability

- **Early Church Model.** Acts records the believers' shared life: "They devoted themselves to the apostles' teaching and the fellowship, to the breaking of bread and the prayers… And the Lord added to their number day by day those who were being saved" (Acts 2:42, 47). That fellowship was more than social—it was a soul-anchoring network of encouragement and correction.
- **"Iron Sharpens Iron."** Solomon notes, "Iron sharpens iron, and one man sharpens another" (Prov 27:17). Healthy friendships confront sin, rejoice in righteousness, and spur spiritual growth.
- **Mutual Suffering & Joy.** Paul calls believers to "Rejoice with those who rejoice, weep with those who weep" (Rom 12:15). Such emotional resonance deepens our bonds, knitting our hearts in Christ.
- **Boundaries & Blessings.** Unlike ungodly ties (3.2), these friendships are grounded in biblical love—not manipulation or dependency.

3.1.4 Family Covenantal Ties

- **Parent–Child Bonds.** Ephesians 6:1–4 commands children to obey and fathers (and mothers) to nurture "in the Lord"—illustrating a soul tie that teaches faith across generations.
- **Sibling Fellowship.** The early Christians addressed one another as "brothers and sisters" (1 Pet 1:22), forging a spiritual siblinghood that transcended ethnic and social divisions.

- **Extended Family as Gospel Context.** Naomi and Ruth's bond—"Where you go I will go... your people shall be my people" (Ruth 1:16)—shows that family soul ties can extend by covenant choice, modeling God's adopted-children language (Gal 4:5).

3.2 Ungodly Soul Ties

When a bond violates God's design—whether through sin, manipulation, or idolatry—it becomes an ungodly soul tie: a chain that keeps us from walking in freedom.

3.2.1 Sexual & Marital Betrayal

- **One Flesh with Prostitution.** Paul warns, "He who joins himself to a prostitute becomes one body with her" (1 Cor 6:16). Any sexual union outside covenant marriage forges a bond on par with Scripture's highest intimacy—yet without God's blessing, it carries defilement (Heb 13:4).
- **Adultery's Chains.** David's affair with Bathsheba and the resultant consequences (2 Sam 11–12) reveal how an illicit soul tie can trigger a cascade of sin—deceit, murder, and familial turmoil.
- **Pornography & Digital Sexuality.** Though not explicit in Scripture, the same principle applies: repeated mental and emotional immersion in sexual fantasy crafts a powerful tie that enslaves thoughts and triggers compulsive behavior (Matt 5:28).

3.2.2 Codependent & Toxic Friendships

- **Unequally Yoked.** Paul's injunction, "Do not be unequally yoked with unbelievers," warns that deep alliances with those outside Christ can compromise faith (2 Cor 6:14).
- **Bad Company Corrupts.** "Do not be deceived: 'Bad company ruins good morals'" (1 Cor 15:33). Toxic friends may encourage sin, sow discord, or trample our conscience.

- **Manipulative Bonds.** Emotional manipulators tie us to guilt, shame, or fear—tools that hinder spiritual growth (Prov 18:7). Such ties often masquerade as "love" but demand control.

3.2.3 Occultic & Idolatrous Bonds

- **Family Witchcraft.** Israel's cycles of idolatry often began in households: Asa's grandmother Maacah made an abominable idol (1 Kings 15:13). Generational spirit ties—curses or curses invoked—can cling to families.
- **Bondage by Sorcery.** Paul confronts the slave girl possessed by a spirit of divination (Acts 16:16–18); her owners profited from her occultic connection. Believers can become unwittingly entangled in such spirit-tied commerce.
- **Redemptive Break.** Isaiah promises, "No pagan who burns incense to [idols] shall be called among you" (Isa 66:17), pointing to God's ability to sever occultic ties.

3.2.4 Emotional Abuse & Manipulative Relationships

- **Controlling Partnerships.** Relationships that demand obedience under threat, guilt, or shame reflect a soul tie based on power, not love (Gal 5:1).
- **Spiritual Abuse.** Leaders who use Scripture to manipulate—demanding loyalty above Christ—forge toxic soul bonds. Jesus warns of false shepherds who "devour the sheep" (Matt 7:15).
- **Breaking Free.** Peter exhorts, "Grow in the grace and knowledge of our Lord… to him be glory" (2 Pet 3:18). Christ's grace empowers us to renounce manipulative ties.

3.3 Neutral or Seasonal Soul Ties

Not every soul tie is clearly godly or ungodly. Many relationships serve a purpose for a time—then shift or fade.

These **neutral or seasonal** ties require wisdom to manage well.

3.3.1 Family Transitions & Launching Children

- **Empty-Nest Dynamics.** When adult children leave home, parent–child soul ties shift. Parents must release control while remain a source of prayerful support (Phil 2:12–13).
- **Young-Adult Friendships.** College roommates or early-career mentors can form deep ties that later loosen as life stages change. Recognizing the seasonality helps prevent resentments.

3.3.2 Workplace & Ministry Partnerships

- **Team-Based Bonds.** Colleagues share wins, deadlines, and prayers—forming ties that fuel productivity and gospel witness.
- **Project-Based Covenants.** Short-term mission teams or church-plant cohorts may have intense soul-linking for six months or a year; wise leaders debrief and help participants transition when the season ends (Eccl 3:1).

3.3.3 Community & Cultural Connections

- **Neighborhood Networks.** Long-term residents build ties of hospitality and intercession. Such bonds can be leveraged for evangelism (Acts 5 – 6).
- **Affinity Groups.** Hobby or interest groups (sports leagues, book clubs) form neutral soul ties. Though not spiritual covenants, they shape identity and habits.

3.3.4 Digital & Social-Media Ties

- **Online Communities.** Virtual soul ties—prayer groups, social-media friendships—can encourage faith but also foster unhealthy comparisons or envy (Prov 14:30). Manage these ties with discernment:

moderate engagement and cultivate real-life accountability.

3.4 Discerning the Category of a Soul Tie

Given this taxonomy, how do you tell which category a given bond belongs to? Consider three diagnostic questions:

1. **Does it honor Christ's lordship?** Any tie that leads you toward obedience, humility, and love likely belongs to the **Godly** category.
2. **Does it foster bondage or sin?** Ties that trigger guilt, compromise your witness, or enslave your emotions are almost certainly **Ungodly**.
3. **Is it time-bound or context-limited?** Relationships that serve a seasonal or functional role—without deep covenant commitment—are **Neutral** but still warrant healthy boundaries.

By mapping each significant bond in your life against these criteria—and grounding your evaluation in Scripture—you gain clarity about where to invest, where to walk away, and where to establish protective guardrails.

Chapter 4 – How Soul Ties Are Formed

The invisible threads that bind one soul to another often begin with seemingly ordinary encounters—an intimate moment, a shared hardship, a solemn vow. Over time, those encounters can weave into deep, sometimes unbreakable cords that shape emotions, thoughts, and spiritual trajectories. In this chapter, we'll examine **three primary avenues** through which soul ties are formed: **physical unity**, **emotional & psychological doors**, and **spiritual & covenantal doors**. Each pathway will be explored in detail, with biblical illustrations and practical insights, equipping you to recognize how ties take root beneath the surface of everyday life.

4.1 Physical Unity

Physical union carries a weight beyond bodily contact. In Scripture, the body is not merely flesh and blood; it is the temple of the Holy Spirit (1 Cor 6:19–20) and the means by which we express covenant commitment (Gen 2:24). When two people share their bodies—whether in sexual intimacy or in times of trauma—their souls can become intricately knotted together.

4.1.1 Sexual Intimacy

The One-Flesh Principle

From the beginning, God designed sexual union to create a profound bond. Genesis 2:24 declares, "Therefore a man shall leave his father and his mother and hold fast to his wife, and they shall become one flesh." The Hebrew verb *dābaq* (hold fast) connotes clinging or cleaving—an intentional, covenantal adhesion. Though God's design was for marriage, the same physiological and spiritual mechanisms are at work whenever sexual intimacy occurs outside that covenant (1 Cor 6:16–17).

- **Neurochemical Bonds.** Modern neuroscience confirms that during sexual activity the brain releases oxytocin and vasopressin—hormones linked to attachment and trust. While these chemicals serve marriage by deepening affection, they can also cement ties in illicit or premature encounters, leaving one vulnerable to emotional enslavement.
- **Spiritual Resonance.** Paul warns that sexual union with a prostitute makes the two "one body," risking a spiritual tie that contradicts our primary union with Christ (1 Cor 6:16–17). Even after repentance, memories and emotional triggers may linger, requiring intentional deliverance (Heb 13:4).
- **Healing the Wounds.** For those bound by past sexual sins, Scripture offers hope: Christ's blood cleanses "from all unrighteousness" (1 John 1:9) and sets us free "to serve in the new way of the Spirit, and not in the old way of the written code" (Rom 7:6). Inner-healing prayer and counseling can help disentangle the soul from residual shame and unhealthy longing.

Covenant vs. Contract

Marriage is more than a legal contract; it is a covenant before God. Ecclesiastes 5:4–5 underscores the gravity of vows: "When you make a vow to God, do not delay to fulfill it, for he has no pleasure in fools." Entering sexual intimacy without the framework of covenant vows binds souls in a way the Lord never intended, leaving no divine promise to uphold or protect the bond.

- **Protective Boundaries.** Scripture repeatedly calls us to guard our bodies and hearts: "Flee from sexual immorality" (1 Cor 6:18) and "Keep yourself pure" (1 Tim 5:22). Such boundaries honor God's design and prevent the formation of ungodly soul ties that require later severing.

4.1.2 Shared Bodily Trauma

Trauma's Unseen Bonds

When two or more people endure physical suffering or fear together, their souls can become linked in deep solidarity. Bible narratives and modern observations alike reveal how shared trauma forges powerful connections.

- **Biblical Precedent.** David's mighty men who fought alongside him (2 Sam 23:8–39) formed bonds of loyalty so strong that they risked life and limb to protect him. Though these ties were godly, they illustrate how battlefield trauma knits hearts together.
- **Job and His Friends.** When Job sat "among the ashes" mourning loss, his friends sat with him seven days and nights in silence (Job 2:13). Their willingness to share in his bodily and emotional agony created a soul tie of compassion—though later marred by misguided counsel, it began in genuine solidarity.

- **Fight-or-Flight Synchrony.** Research shows that individuals who experience life-threatening events together can develop synchronized stress responses, cementing an unspoken bond. Spiritually, this may manifest as a sense of "we've been through this together," compelling survivors to cling to one another for comfort (Eccl 4:9–12).
- **Idolatry of the Shared Past.** While communal support is vital, there is danger if one idolizes the trauma bond. Holding too tightly to the past can prevent moving forward in Christ. The Lord calls us to "forget what lies behind and strain forward to what lies ahead" (Phil 3:13).

Paths to Healthy Commemoration

- **Redemptive Memory.** Remembering shared suffering can foster gratitude for God's deliverance. Celebrate milestones of healing together—such as anniversaries of rescue or recovery—while acknowledging that ultimate security rests in Christ (Rom 8:18).
- **Setting Emotional Boundaries.** Trauma bonds require careful shepherding. Encourage survivors to broaden support networks beyond the immediate group, preventing an exclusive tie that isolates them from the wider body of Christ (Heb 10:24–25).

4.2 Emotional & Psychological Doors

Beyond the physical, soul ties often form through emotional resonance—when hearts open wide to another's joys or sorrows. While empathy and vulnerability foster intimacy, they can also slip into unhealthy enmeshment.

The Gift and Risk of Empathy

Jesus exemplified perfect empathy: He wept with Mary and Martha over Lazarus (John 11:35) and felt compassion for the crowds (Matt 9:36). However, when empathy lacks proper boundaries, it can draw one soul too deeply into another's inner world.

- **Emotional Flooding.** Intense sharing of feelings—grief, anger, fear—releases neurochemicals that synchronize brainwaves, creating a kind of emotional resonance. In safe, timely doses, this builds trust; in excess, it can lead to emotional fusion, where one person's emotions become inextricable from another's.
- **Codependency.** A codependent friendship or partnership arises when one person's sense of worth or identity becomes tied to meeting another's emotional needs. Proverbs 18:1 warns, "Whoever isolates himself seeks his own desire… he breaks out against all sound judgment." True empathy builds life; codependency drains it.

Biblical Examples and Warnings

- **Naomi & Ruth.** Ruth's famous pledge to Naomi—"Where you go I will go" (Ruth 1:16)—exemplifies healthy, sacrificial empathy grounded in covenant loyalty. Yet the narrative remains balanced: Ruth gains identity not by losing herself, but by embracing Naomi's God as her God (Ruth 1:16–17).
- **Mary Magdalene and the Chief Priests.** After the crucifixion, Mary became consumed with sorrow. The religious leaders demanded she prove her tears by naming alliances (Matt 27:61; Luke 8:2). Though her grief forged bonds of solidarity with other women, it did not entangle her in theological debates—she remained focused on Christ's resurrection (John 20:11–18).

Nurturing Healthy Emotional Ties

- **Self-Awareness in Vulnerability.** Scripture calls us to "guard our hearts" (Prov 4:23). Before disclosing deeply, ask, "Am I seeking mutual support or escape from my own pain?"
- **Mutual Encouragement.** Paul's exhortation, "Comfort each other and edify one another" (1 Thess 5:11), envisions empathy as reciprocal—each party both gives and receives, maintaining emotional balance.
- **Professional Support.** Some emotional wounds require counselor or pastoral care intervention. A trained third party can help disentangle codependent patterns and guide toward Christ-centered wholeness.

4.3 Spiritual & Covenantal Doors

The deepest soul ties often form in spiritual arenas: through vows, rituals, or shared encounters with the divine. These ties can be benign—such as baptism and communion—or treacherous—such as occultic pacts.

4.3.1 Oaths, Vows, and Rituals

Biblical Foundations of Vow-Making

- **Vows as Covenant Seals.** In Israel, making a vow before God created a binding spiritual bond. Numbers 30 outlines laws governing vows, emphasizing their seriousness: "When a young woman makes a vow... her father may confirm or nullify it" (Num 30:3–16).
- **Nazirite Vow.** Those who took the Nazirite vow consecrated themselves by abstaining from wine, avoiding the dead, and not cutting hair (Num 6:1–21). Their bodies and souls were set apart in a visible, spiritual tie to God for a time.
- **New Testament Warnings.** Jesus cautioned, "Do not take an oath at all... Let what you say be simply 'Yes' or 'No'" (Matt 5:34–37), highlighting how easily human

vows can become empty or hypocritical when divorced from a heart submitted to God.

Formation of Soul Ties Through Rituals

- **Christian Initiations.** Baptism and the Lord's Supper are covenantal rituals that bind believers to Christ and one another. While these ties are meant for life, they require ongoing participation and faith to remain vital (Rom 6:3–5; 1 Cor 11:23–26).
- **Occultic Initiations.** Conversely, secret societies or pagan cults often employ blood oaths, symbolic scarification, or repetitive chants to forge a spiritual tie with demonic powers. Acts 19:19 records that new believers "brought their books together and burned them"—renouncing such ties.

Breaking or Honoring Spiritual Vows

- **Renouncing Ungodly Pacts.** Scripture provides a model in Jehoshaphat's reforms: "Remove the foreign altars and the high places… and command Judah to seek the LORD" (2 Chron 17:6). Declaring, "I renounce all vows and pacts contrary to Christ," in prayer is a first step to sever spiritual ties.
- **Reaffirming Godly Covenants.** At renewal times— weddings, baptisms, Reformation anniversaries— believers publicly recommit to the vows made before God, thereby strengthening the soul tie to Christ and the body (Ps 50:5).

4.4 Additional Pathways to Formation

Although our primary categories (physical, emotional, spiritual) encompass most soul-tie formations, two more avenues deserve brief attention: **shared mission** and **fear-based bonding**.

4.4.1 Shared Mission & Sacrifice

- **Acts 2's Communal Life.** The earliest church "had all things in common" (Acts 2:44–45). Risking livelihood to serve the poor created a powerful bond among believers, akin to troops sharing supply lines in war.
- **Martyrdom Bonds.** When Christians face persecution together, their unity in suffering mirrors Christ's own path (Rev 2:10). Those who survive often report lifelong soul ties with fellow sufferers.

4.4.2 Fear & Control as Bonding Agents

- **Manipulative Churches.** Cults exploit fear—of hell, of rejection, of curses—to bind members' souls to the group. Such fear-based ties bypass genuine love and cloak bondage in religious language (2 Tim 3:1–5).
- **Healing Through Truth.** The antidote to fear is "sound doctrine" and the promise that "perfect love casts out fear" (2 Tim 1:13–14; 1 John 4:18). Replacing fear-driven vows with love-driven trust frees the soul.

Chapter 5 – Discernment: Signs & Symptoms

Discernment is the spiritual skill of "seeing" beneath the surface—the ability to recognize when a soul tie is at work in your life and to distinguish godly bonds from entangling chains. Without discernment, even well-meaning relationships can carry hidden costs: subtle shifts in priorities, renewed cycles of guilt, or unnoticed compromises in holiness. In this chapter, we'll explore in-depth the **behavioral**, **emotional**, and **spiritual** indicators that signal a soul tie—whether healthy or harmful. By learning these signs and symptoms, you'll be equipped to name what's happening in your heart, bring it to Christ in prayer, and take wise next steps.

5.1 Behavioral Indicators

Behavior—what we do—often betrays the unseen knots in our souls before we even realize they exist. When a relationship has forged a soul tie, certain **patterns of choice and conduct** begin to emerge. Pay attention to the following behavioral symptoms.

5.1.1 Compulsive Preoccupation

Description. You find your thoughts drifting to a person at inopportune times—during work, prayer, or family conversations—and struggle to redirect your mind elsewhere.

- **Biblical parallel.** Solomon warns against fixating on forbidden pleasures: "My beloved had put his hand to the latch, and my heart was thrilling within me" (Song 5:4). Though here the text celebrates marital love, the same language illustrates how preoccupation can seize the heart.
- **Key questions.**
    1. How often do thoughts of this person interrupt your daily responsibilities?
    2. Do you catch yourself daydreaming about him or her more than once an hour?
- **Spiritual risk.** Compulsive preoccupation often points to an ungodly tie—especially if your mind cycles through memories of conflict, guilt, or longing, rather than healthy affection or gratitude.

5.1.2 Impaired Boundaries

Description. You find it difficult to say "no," even when requests from this person violate your values, exhaust your time, or hurt other relationships.

- **Biblical principle.** Jesus occasionally withdrew from the crowds to pray alone (Mark 1:35)—a model of necessary boundaries.
- **Red-flag behaviors.**
    o Canceling personal plans to meet their demands.
    o Lending money or resources despite repeated misuse.
    o Ignoring your spouse's or family's needs because this relationship "needs" you more.
- **Warning sign.** When saying "yes" violates your conscience or depletes your spiritual resources, the

bond has become a controlling tie rather than a mutual one.

5.1.3 Pattern of Repetitive Choices

Description. You repeatedly find yourself returning to the same unhealthy dynamic—re-igniting conflict, emotional codependency, or secret communication—even after promising yourself you'll break free.

- **Scriptural reminder.** Paul writes, "For the good that I would, I do not; but the evil which I would not, that I practice" (Rom 7:19). While this conflict is universal to fallen humanity, a **soultie** magnifies it, dragging you back into patterns long after they cease serving you.
- **Examples.**
  - Sending late-night texts after a breakup, despite experiencing regret each morning.
  - Returning to a friend or mentor who habitually demeans or manipulates you.
- **Implication.** Such repetitive choices betray a tie that exercises undue power over your will. Recognizing the pattern is the first step toward interrupting it.

5.1.4 Withdrawal from Community

Description. You feel uncomfortable or resentful when receiving love, counsel, or accountability from other believers—because your strongest loyalty lies with this one soul tie.

- **New Testament example.** When Peter denied Christ, his shame likely drove him into isolation—even as other disciples remained together (Mk 14:66–72). While not a soul tie in the romantic sense, his fear-driven withdrawal illustrates the impulse to isolate around a harmful bond.
- **Behavioral symptoms.**
  - Reluctance to attend small groups or meet with mentors.

- o Defensiveness when others ask about the relationship.
  - o A sense of "they just don't understand" fueling your alienation.
- **Spiritual cost.** A healthy soul tie draws you deeper into the body of Christ; an unhealthy one drives you away, cutting you off from sources of prayer, wisdom, and grace.

5.2 Emotional Indicators

Our emotions serve as God-given barometers of intimacy: joy, sorrow, anger, and fear can signal how deeply a bond has touched us. But when emotions spiral beyond healthy ranges—or persist long after the relationship has ended—they point to a soul tie that needs discernment.

5.2.1 Unexplained Guilt or Shame

Description. You carry a heavy sense of remorse or self-reproach connected to the relationship—often without conscious sin to confess in the present moment.

- **Biblical reference.** Isaiah prophesies of Christ, "He was oppressed, and he was afflicted, yet he opened not his mouth" (Isa 53:7). While Jesus bore guilt for our sake, His shame led to glory. Our own lingering guilt, however, often signals an unresolved bond.
- **Key reflections.**
  1. Does the guilt correspond to ongoing sin, or is it a residual shadow from past choices?
  2. Have you tasted full forgiveness in Christ for those past choices (1 John 1:9)?
- **Next steps.** Bring that residual guilt before the Lord in confession and thanksgiving. If the guilt persists, seek pastoral counsel to identify hidden ties that perpetuate it.

5.2.2 Persistent Longing or Nostalgia

Description. Even when circumstances argue against reconnection, you find yourself longing for the "good times" or imagining a different ending.

- **Song of Solomon lens.** The bride remembers her beloved: "I opened to my beloved, but my beloved had turned and gone..." (Song 5:6). The yearning in the poem celebrates marital love; outside that covenant, nostalgia can deceive the heart.
- **Diagnostic questions.**
    o Are you idealizing memories, overlooking the relationship's toxic aspects?
    o Does longing intensify when you're lonely, bored, or stressed?
- **Spiritual warning.** Nostalgia without wisdom becomes a snare—luring you back into a tie that God has called you to release.

5.2.3 Anxiety and Fear Patterns

Description. Thoughts of losing contact or approval from this person provoke anxiety attacks, nightmares, or chronic worry.

- **New Testament example.** Peter's fear of man led to denial; the fear was rooted in attachment to human approval (John 18:15–27).
- **Emotional markers.**
    o Physical sensations: tight chest, racing heart, sweating when you anticipate rejection.
    o Mental loops: "If I don't message them, they'll forget me" or "If I don't comply, they'll be angry."
- **Biblical antidote.** "There is no fear in love, but perfect love casts out fear" (1 John 4:18). When a bond spawns fear instead of love, it has become an idol masquerading as relationship.

5.2.4 Enmeshment and Loss of Self

Description. Your identity, values, or interests shift to match this person's—sometimes unconsciously—and you struggle to articulate your own opinions or desires.

- **Scriptural counterpoint.** Paul declares, "I have been crucified with Christ; it is no longer I who live, but Christ who lives in me" (Gal 2:20). Healthy soul ties support self-giving love, but they do not erase individuality in Christ.
- **Signs of enmeshment.**
  - You finish their sentences mentally.
  - You feel hollow when separated, as though "half" of you went missing.
  - You adopt their moral or political views reflexively, without prayerful reflection.
- **Recovery path.** Reclaim your identity in Christ through guided journaling (see Chapter 12), asking, "Who am I in Christ apart from this bond?" and surrounding yourself with affirming, godly community.

5.3 Spiritual Indicators

Beyond behavior and emotion, soul ties register in our **spiritual experience**—our prayer life, worship, and sense of calling. When a tie is healthy, it draws us nearer to God; when it is ungodly, it creates spiritual friction or dryness.

5.3.1 Hindrance in Prayer Life

Description. You struggle to pray openly or deeply when alone with the Lord—your thoughts circle back to the soul tie, leaving you restless or distracted.

- **Jesus' model.** He "withdrew to lonely places and prayed" regularly (Luke 5:16). Regular communion with God requires freedom to focus wholly on Him.
- **Symptom analysis.**

- You pray only shallow prayers or uniform petitions about that person ("Bless them, Lord..."), rather than seeking God's agenda.
- You feel guilty for not praying for them enough, turning prayer into another task of obligation.
- **Spiritual remedy.** Practice the **Jesus Prayer** ("Lord Jesus Christ, Son of God, have mercy on me") to recenter your heart (Phil 4:6–7). If praying for this person feels compulsive, bring it before a trusted mentor for guidance.

5.3.2 Spiritual Dryness and Despair

Description. A pervasive sense of spiritual emptiness or aimlessness follows the tie—you wonder if God is distant or indifferent.

- **Psalms of lament.** David's cries, "Why are you cast down, O my soul?" (Ps 42:5, 11), capture the ache of spiritual drought. While lament itself is a godly response, perpetual dryness often means an ungodly tie is siphoning your joy.
- **Indicators.**
  - You stop enjoying prayer, worship, or Scripture.
  - You feel numb to spiritual joys—no tears in repentance or joy in thanksgiving.
- **Step toward refreshment.** Revisit **Psalm 63** and reclaim the language of thirst for God. Fast from all contact with the tied relationship for a set period (e.g., a week), using the time to feast on God's presence.

5.3.3 Disruption of Vision and Direction

Description. You once sensed clear direction about ministry, or spiritual gifts—but now feel foggy or doubting.

- **Biblical illustration.** Gideon received clear commissioning from an angel (Judg 6:12–14), then faltered under fear. His wavering shows how doubt can overtake calling when faith is displaced.

- **Diagnostic prompts.**
  - Do you question God's calling more when the person enters your mind?
  - Does their approval seem linked to your sense of worth or purpose?
- **Reorientation.** Return to **Habakkuk 2:2**—"Write the vision; make it plain." Journal the vision God gave you, intercede for clarity, and enlist an accountability partner to pray over it.

5.3.4 Recurring Sin Patterns

Description. Despite genuine repentance, you repeatedly stumble in the same sin tied to the relationship—jealousy, bitterness, lust, or control.

- **Paul's struggle.** He longed to do good but found evil at work within (Rom 7:21). A soul tie intensifies that struggle, keeping the same sin at the fore of temptation.
- **Sin-map approach.** Identify the triggers—what the person says, does, or recalls in you that sparks sin.
- **Freedom strategy.** Use the "3 R's": **Recognize** the trigger, **Repent** in the moment, **Replace** the thought with a Scripture truth (Phil 4:8). Over time, the tie's power will weaken.

Chapter 6 – Consequences of Ungodly Soul Ties

When a soul tie deviates from God's design, it becomes a conduit for dysfunction rather than divine blessing. Ungodly soul ties can warp our sense of self, trap us in recurring patterns of sin, and undermine every healthy relationship around us. In this chapter, we'll examine three major categories of fallout—**distorted identity**, **repetitive sin cycles**, and **relational sabotage**—unpacking how each one plays out in thought, emotion, and behavior. Through Scripture's vivid warnings and promises, we'll learn to recognize these consequences early and seek Christ's healing deliverance.

6.1 Distorted Identity

A primary casualty of an ungodly soul tie is the believer's identity in Christ. When our sense of worth, purpose, or belonging depends on another human connection rather than on our union with Jesus, our self-understanding becomes warped.

6.1.1 Erosion of Self-Worth

Ungodly ties often demand approval or performance in exchange for acceptance. Over time, you may begin to believe your value hinges on pleasing or serving that person.

- **Performance-Based Worth.** In relationships rooted in manipulation or control, affection is conditional. You learn that "I am loved when I do X," instead of "I am loved because I am God's child" (1 John 3:1). This conditional acceptance parallels Israel's temptation to earn God's favor by works rather than resting in His grace (Gal 2:16).
- **Anxiety Over Approval.** The constant pressure to perform triggers chronic anxiety: "If I don't meet their expectations, I'll lose their care." Such anxiety echoes the Pharisees' slavish obedience to rules without experiencing Christ's rest (Matt 11:28–30).
- **Scriptural Antidote.** Psalm 139:14 declares, "I praise you, for I am fearfully and wonderfully made." Rooting your identity in God's creative purpose, rather than another's fickle approval, is step one toward healing.

6.1.2 Confused Identity in Christ

When an ungodly tie becomes the lens through which you view yourself, you lose sight of your true standing in Christ.

- **Lost in the "One Flesh" Lie.** Sexual sin or illicit intimacy can convince you that "we are one," blurring where you end and the other begins (1 Cor 6:16–17). Instead of "I belong to Christ," you feel you belong to that person.
- **Diminished Spiritual Calling.** As your identity narrows to the relationship, your sense of unique gifts and callings fades. God's specific "workmanship" for you (Eph 2:10) dims beneath the shadow of the ungodly tie.
- **Reclamation in Christ.** Galatians 2:20 reminds us, "I have been crucified with Christ; it is no longer I who live, but Christ who lives in me." Rehearse this truth

daily—meditate on your baptismal union with Jesus (Rom 6:3–5) until it restores your God-ward identity.

6.1.3 Identity Masking and Performance

To maintain an unhealthy tie, you may adopt a false persona—hiding your true feelings, convictions, or struggles.

- **Masking True Emotions.** Fear of rejection leads you to suppress grief, anger, or conviction. You say what pleases, not what you believe, mirroring Achan's hidden sin that "devoted" Israel to defeat (Josh 7:1–5).
- **Spiritual Pretense.** You attend church or pray on cue to maintain the connection, rather than from genuine devotion—akin to Pharisaical righteousness that "honors me with lips, but their hearts are far from me" (Isa 29:13).
- **Freedom Through Transparency.** James 5:16 exhorts, "Confess your sins to one another and pray for one another, that you may be healed." True identity blossoms in safe confession, not in the smothering cloak of pretense.

6.2 Repetitive Sin Cycles

Ungodly soul ties often operate like spiritual magnets, pulling us repeatedly into the same sins—lust, manipulation, resentment—long after we've repented.

6.2.1 Bondage to Patterns of Sin

- **The Vicious Loop.** Each time you reconnect with the person or recall the bond, your heart triggers old thought–action sequences: temptation, compromise, guilt, brief relief, then renewed guilt. This mirrors Paul's lament: "For the good I would, I do not; but the evil I would not, that I practice" (Rom 7:19).
- **Emotional Cues as Triggers.** A certain song, location, or anniversary can flood you with desire or anger tied to the relationship. Like Israel's golden calf

ritual responding to Sinai's absence (Ex 32), sensory triggers catalyze idolatrous patterns.

- **Breaking the Cycle.** Identify and avoid strong triggers (Matt 5:29–30). Replace the pattern with positive spiritual habits—praying Psalm 51 when guilt strikes, calling a mentor instead of texting the ex, and fasting from reminders until freedom grows.

6.2.2 Legalistic Religion and False Guilt

- **Works-Based Repentance.** Some respond to repetitive sin by doubling down on religion—more fasting, extra prayers, rigid rule-keeping—hoping to earn relief from guilt. This echoes Saul's perfectionism that drove David into refuge (1 Sam 18:10–11) but never satisfied.
- **Cycle of Relapse.** When the extra rules inevitably break, guilt intensifies: "I failed again; I must try harder." This self- condemnation contradicts "there is now no condemnation for those who are in Christ Jesus" (Rom 8:1).
- **Grace-Fueled Freedom.** Embrace God's grace as Paul teaches: "The law of the Spirit of life in Christ Jesus has set you free from the law of sin and death" (Rom 8:2). Celebrate grace, not performance, and allow it to fuel your struggle.

6.2.3 Spiritual Oppression and Temptation Amplification

Ungodly soul ties can invite demonic footholds—legal rights for the enemy to harass you spiritually.

- **Uninvited Guests.** Jesus cast out demons only when He had authority and when the person's ties to the demonic realm were broken (Luke 4:18–19). In relationships bound by occultic vows or manipulations, these spiritual attachments persist.
- **Temptation's Intensification.** Once the bond forms, every memory or emotional charge becomes a portal for the enemy to tempt you toward bitterness, lust, or fear (Eph 6:16).

- **Deliverance Path.** Renounce any unholy vows in Christ's name (Matt 16:19), confess shared sins, and bind the enemy's access ("In the name of Jesus, I forbid you"—Luke 10:19). Then fill the vacuum with worship (Ps 100) and Scripture meditation, displacing spiritual darkness with God's light (Ps 119:105).

6.3 Relational Sabotage

Ungodly soul ties rarely remain isolated; they spill over and weaken every other friendship, family bond, and ministry calling.

6.3.1 Breakdown of Trust

- **Secrecy and Deceit.** To protect the unhealthy bond, you may lie or omit the truth—either about the nature of the relationship or your actions to sustain it (Prov 12:22). This pattern erodes your credibility with spouses, friends, and church leaders.
- **Overreactions and Volatility.** When others attempt to intervene, you react defensively—anger, withdrawal, or denial—further fracturing trust. Like King Saul's paranoia driving away advisors (1 Sam 18:8–9), your volatile defense of the tie repels genuine care.
- **Rebuilding Confidence.** True restoration requires transparency: share your struggles publicly with a small group, ask forgiveness for past deceptions (Luke 17:3–4), and invite accountability as proof of changed heart.

6.3.2 Isolation from Healthy Community

- **Alienation of Allies.** As the ungodly tie monopolizes your time and attention, you'll cancel gatherings, ignore calls, and gradually drift from godly peers (Heb 10:24–25).
- **Formation of Cliques.** You may gravitate toward a subculture that normalizes the unhealthy bond—a

gossip circle, a political faction, or a distorted support group—cutting you off from balanced perspectives.

- **Restoration through Community.** Deliberately re-enter broader fellowship. Attend small groups, serve in a ministry team, and choose new accountability partners who reflect Christ's character. Community immersion helps reverse isolation's damage.

6.3.3 Impairment of Ministry and Calling

- **Loss of Focus.** The tie's emotional demands sap your passion and effectiveness in your God-given calling. Your mind wanders during sermons, your prayers become perfunctory, and your service feels burdensome.
- **Compromised Witness.** Outsiders notice when your life isn't aligned with your message. A teacher who preaches purity yet clings to an illicit bond undermines the gospel's credibility (Matt 5:16).
- **Recommissioning by Grace.** Romans 12:1–2 calls us to present our bodies as living sacrifices and to be transformed by renewing our minds. Return your ministry and gifts to the Lord—offer them afresh as acts of worship—and let Him re-energize your calling apart from the ungodly tie.

Chapter 7 – Breaking Unhealthy Soul Ties

In Christ we have been called to freedom: "For freedom Christ has set us free; stand firm therefore, and do not submit again to a yoke of slavery" (Gal 5:1). Yet when an unhealthy soul tie grips our hearts, it feels as though chains of guilt, fear, or compulsion hold us fast. Breaking such ties requires more than sheer willpower—it demands spiritual strategies rooted in repentance, renunciation, deliverance, inner healing, and the establishment of wise boundaries. In this chapter, we'll walk step by step through the processes that lead from bondage to breakthrough, drawing on biblical precedent and practical ministry models to guide you into the liberty Jesus purchased.

7.1 Repentance & Renunciation

True freedom always begins with repentance—turning away from the sin or misplaced allegiance that fueled the soul tie—and renunciation—publicly rejecting every vow, curse, or commitment that gave the tie spiritual authority.

Biblical Foundation. The apostle John assures us: "If we confess our sins, he is faithful and just to forgive us our sins and to cleanse us from all unrighteousness" (1 John 1:9). Similarly, David modeled heartfelt repentance when confronted with his sin against Bathsheba: "Against you, you only, have I sinned and done what is evil in your sight… Create in me a clean heart, O God" (Psalm 51:4, 10).

Steps to Genuine Repentance.

1. **Acknowledgment.** Identify the specific sin(s) or unhealthy allegiance—be it sexual immorality, codependency, occult entanglement, or ongoing bitterness—that undergirded the tie.
2. **Godward Confession.** Speak honestly to the Lord: "Father, I confess that I allowed [name/behavior] to dominate my heart and led me into bondage." Use Psalm 32:5 as your pattern: "I acknowledged my sin to you… and you forgave the iniquity of my sin."
3. **Restitution Where Possible.** If your tie involved harm to another—lies, manipulation, financial misuse—take concrete steps to make amends (Luke 19:8). Even if full restoration isn't possible, express your desire for reconciliation before God.
4. **Repentance Prayer.** Craft or use a prayer of repentance: "Lord Jesus, I turn from this bond. I renounce every thought, word, and action that has tied my soul. Forgive me, cleanse me, and restore me by Your blood."

Spiritual Fruit. Genuine repentance loosens the spiritual authority that sin grants the enemy (Eph 4:27). As you confess and turn, God's forgiveness breaks the controlling power of that sin-pattern in your life.

7.1.2 Renunciation Prayers

Why Renunciation? Many soul ties carry spiritual rights—vows sworn, curses spoken, rituals performed—that enable demonic or ungodly forces to maintain access. Renunciation prayers explicitly revoke these rights.

Key Bible Passages.

- **Ephesians 6:12–13:** "For we do not wrestle against flesh and blood… Therefore take up the whole armor of God… that you may be able to withstand in the evil day." Spiritual warfare requires naming and nullifying the enemy's footholds.
- **Jeremiah 4:14:** "O Jerusalem, wash your heart from wickedness, that you may be saved. How long shall your evil thoughts lodge within you?" Washing one's heart includes renunciation.

Components of a Renunciation Prayer.

1. **Identification.** Speak clearly: "In the name of Jesus, I renounce every vow I have made to [person/occult power] that bound my soul."
2. **Repudiation.** "I revoke all curses, oaths, or agreements made knowingly or unknowingly that granted any spiritual right over my life."
3. **Cleansing Declaration.** "By the blood of Jesus, I am cleansed from all sin, all debt, and all unholy obligations."
4. **Commissioning of Light.** "I invite the Holy Spirit to fill every place the enemy once occupied, and I declare that only the Lord God Almighty has authority in my heart."

Practical Tips.

- Speak out loud—vocalizing your renunciation activates your faith (Rom 10:17).
- Use Scripture within your prayer (e.g., "It is for freedom that Christ has set us free" – Gal 5:1).
- If you find multiple ties (sexual, emotional, occultic), pray separately over each category for clarity and thoroughness.

Understanding Generational Bonds. Ungodly patterns can transmit through families: abuse, addiction, occult involvement. Exodus 20:5 warns, "Visiting the iniquity of the fathers on the children to the third and the fourth generation." Yet Galatians 3:13 proclaims, "Christ redeemed us from… the curse of the law, having become a curse for us."

Steps for Generational Renunciation.

1. **Identify Patterns.** Prayerfully survey your family history—look for recurring struggles (e.g., alcoholism, spiritualism, sexual abuse).
2. **Intercessory Confession.** On behalf of ancestors, pray: "Lord, forgive my family line for [specific sins]. I renounce every legal right the enemy has gained through these transgressions."
3. **Claiming Redemption.** Declare Galatians 3:13: "Christ has redeemed me from every generational curse."
4. **Seal with Thanksgiving.** Thank God for breaking the cycle and setting you free (Psalm 103:2–3).

Ongoing Vigilance. Generational curses may express subtly—through repeated sin tendencies or health issues. If triggers resurface, revisit your family renunciation prayers and seek pastoral deliverance prayer.

7.1.4 Forgiveness of Others and Self

Why Forgiveness Matters. Unforgiveness preserves ties: bitterness toward another person often feels like loyalty to them. Jesus insisted: "If you do not forgive others their trespasses, neither will your Father forgive your trespasses" (Matt 6:15).

Forgiving Others.

- **Step 1: Acknowledge Hurt.** Name the offenses: "I was hurt when [name] did [action]."

- **Step 2: Choose to Forgive.** "In obedience to Christ, I choose to forgive [name] for [offense]. I release them into God's hands."
- **Step 3: Pray Blessings.** "Father, bless [name] and draw them to Yourself." (Luke 6:28).
- **Step 4: Release Attachment.** Intentionally withdraw emotional energy from the offense—resist rehearsing pain.

Forgiving Self.

- **Confession to God.** "Lord, I confess my part in the sin—the times I enabled or participated in this bond."
- **Receiving Grace.** Meditate on Romans 8:1: "There is therefore now no condemnation for those who are in Christ Jesus." Let Scripture replace guilt-laden thoughts.
- **Self-Compassion through Christ.** Recognize that Christ's love covers your shame; treat yourself with the same mercy you extend to others (Eph 4:32).

7.2 Deliverance & Inner-Healing Models

While repentance and renunciation break legal authority, true freedom often requires **deliverance ministry** and **inner-healing** work to restore wounded parts of the soul.

7.2.1 Exercising Authority in Christ

Biblical Mandate. Jesus granted believers authority over demonic powers: "Behold, I give you authority to tread on serpents and scorpions… and nothing shall hurt you" (Luke 10:19). Similarly, Mark 16:17 promises, "They will cast out demons in my name."

Practical Application.

1. **Position in Christ.** Begin by affirming your identity: "I am a child of God, seated with Christ in heavenly places" (Eph 2:6).

2. **Command by Name.** In prayer, identify the spirit or bond: "In the name of Jesus, I command the spirit of [fear, lust, control] to leave me now."
3. **Use Scripture as Sword.** Quote relevant passages: "Your word is a lamp to my feet" (Ps 119:105) or "Submit yourselves therefore to God; resist the devil, and he will flee from you" (James 4:7).
4. **Act in Faith.** Deliverance prayers should be spoken with conviction. If you feel peace descend, rejoice; if not, continue until you sense breakthrough.

Team Ministry. For deep-rooted ties, enlist mature believers or a qualified deliverance minister. Corporate authority amplifies effect: "Again, truly I say to you, if two of you agree on earth about anything... it will be done for them by my Father" (Matt 18:19).

7.2.2 Prayer Models for Deliverance

Model A: The Four-Step Deliverance Prayer

1. **Adoration & Thanksgiving.** Begin by exalting God's supremacy (Ps 95:6).
2. **Confession & Renunciation.** As in §7.1, confess sin and renounce ties.
3. **Command & Expel.** Speak directly: "I command every ungodly soul tie to break now by the blood of Jesus."
4. **Commission Holy Presence.** "Holy Spirit, fill me anew. Heal every wound and seal me as Christ's own."

Model B: The Healing Rooms Approach

- **Encounter with Jesus.** Visualize Christ's presence, allowing Him to reveal hidden wounds (Rev 3:20).
- **Inner-Healing Dialogue.** Speak to wounded parts of your soul: "I release you from the lie you believed."
- **Release & Replace.** Forgive yourself, receive God's truth, and thank Jesus for His redemptive work (Phil 4:8).

Why Inner-Healing? Unhealthy soul ties often leave emotional and psychological scars—shame, fear, rejection—that must be healed before new bonds can flourish.

Key Components.

1. **Identifying Wounds.** Through journaling or guided questions, uncover root experiences: "When did I first feel unworthy of love?"
2. **Processing Emotions.** Allow the Holy Spirit to surface grief, anger, or fear in a safe context—small group, counselor, or prayer ministry.
3. **Applying Scripture.** Counter each lie with biblical truth: e.g., "I am a child of God" (John 1:12) replaces "I am unlovable."
4. **Releasing the Past.** Symbolic actions—tearing vow documents, washing hands—help the mind internalize spiritual realities (Is 44:22).

Biblical Assurance. "He heals the brokenhearted and binds up their wounds" (Psalm 147:3). Healing inner wounds resets the soil of your soul, preparing it for healthy, godly ties.

7.2.4 Role of the Holy Spirit in Healing

Divine Healer. Jesus promised the Comforter: "He will teach you all things and bring to your remembrance all that I have said to you" (John 14:26). The Spirit brings understanding of how ties formed and guides you into truth.

Practices.

- **Listening Prayer.** Quiet your heart and listen for the Spirit's voice—He may pinpoint a memory or lie needing release (1 Cor 2:10).
- **Spiritual Gifts.** Healer and word-of-knowledge gifts can surface hidden bond points in corporate settings (1 Cor 12:9, 10).

- **Continuous Filling.** Regularly ask, "Fill me anew, Holy Spirit," to maintain Christ's authority in your heart (Eph 5:18).

7.2.5 Professional Help: Pastoral Counseling & Therapy

When to Seek Help. If trauma bonds stem from abuse, PTSD, or deep psychological wounds, professional intervention—Christian counselor or psychologist—may be essential.

Integration of Faith and Psychology.

- **Biblical Counsel.** Pastoral counselors use Scripture for direction and prayer support.
- **Clinical Tools.** Therapists employ evidence-based techniques (CBT, EMDR) to rewire trauma pathways.
- **Collaborative Care.** An integrated approach respects both spiritual deliverance and mental-health expertise, ensuring holistic freedom.

7.3 Establishing Boundaries

Breaking ties clears the way for new habits—but without healthy boundaries, old patterns and new temptations will rush back. Boundaries safeguard freedom, honor relationships, and cultivate spiritual growth.

7.3.1 Scriptural Basis for Boundaries

God Sets Boundaries. The Creator defined limits in Eden—"You may surely eat of every tree of the garden, but of the tree of the knowledge of good and evil you shall not eat" (Gen 2:16–17). **Wisdom Literature.** "Above all else, guard your heart, for everything you do flows from it" (Prov 4:23). Guarding implies active boundary-making.

7.3.2 Types of Boundaries

1. **Physical Boundaries.**

- Limiting contact or distance: no unaccompanied meetings, no shared living spaces, or breaking off physical intimacy entirely (2 Cor 6:17).
2. **Emotional Boundaries.**
   - Restricting emotional disclosure: deciding what you will or won't share to prevent re-opening old wounds.
3. **Spiritual Boundaries.**
   - Avoiding joint prayer/ministry with the person until freedom is secured, removing them from prayer chains or accountability circles (Matt 18:15–17).

7.3.3 Practical Steps to Set Boundaries

Communicate Clearly. Use "I" statements: "I need time apart so I can heal." **Be Consistent.** Enforce boundary each time it's tested—consistency builds new neural pathways (Heb 10:24–25). **Use Technology Wisely.** Block screens, mute notifications, or delete contact information to prevent impulsive outreach. **Safe Distance vs. Total Cut-Off.**

- **Safe Distance.** Partial restriction allows limited, controlled interaction (e.g., work context) while protecting your core vulnerability.
- **Total Cut-Off.** In cases of abuse or persistent manipulation, complete separation may be required for safety (Prov 22:3).

7.3.4 Maintaining Boundaries and Accountability

Accountability Partnerships. Invite a mature believer to check in regularly—text or call them before deciding to reach out to the person you've separated from. **Church Community.** Engage in small groups, serve in ministry, and cultivate new godly friendships that affirm your worth in Christ. **Ongoing Prayer.** Pray daily for strength to maintain boundaries: "Lord, empower me by Your Spirit to stand firm in the liberty You have given me" (Gal 5:1).

7.3.5 Loving but Wise Boundaries

Boundaries are not walls of resentment but hedges of love—protective measures that preserve both hearts. Jesus commanded us to love our neighbors as ourselves (Mark 12:31); learning to love with wisdom means sometimes saying "no" to unhealthy ties so you can say "yes" to God's best relationships.

Chapter 8 – Healing & Restoration After Severance

When an ungodly soul tie is broken, the aftermath often feels like a wound—raw, tender, and in need of careful healing. Though breaking the bond was necessary, the heart remains bruised, the mind cluttered with memories, and the spirit yearning for wholeness. This chapter walks you through the journey from severance to restoration, grounded in biblical truth and enriched by practical disciplines. We'll explore how to **grieve well**, **rebuild self-worth in Christ**, and **engage community and accountability** so that the Lord's promise— "He heals the brokenhearted and binds up their wounds" (Psalm 147:3)—becomes your lived reality.

8.1 Grieving the Loss of a Bond

Severing a soul tie is not merely a decision; it is a loss. Just as one grieves a death, so the heart must mourn what once was—hopes, shared dreams, and a sense of mutual belonging. Grieving is not weakness but a God-given pathway to healing.

8.1.1 Recognizing the Need to Grieve

Before we can heal, we must admit the depth of our loss. Denial only prolongs pain.

- **Acknowledge the Void.** The sudden absence of phone calls, texts, or shared routines leaves a silence that echoes in your soul. Admit the pain: "I feel lost without this connection."
- **Understand Biblical Grief.** In Ecclesiastes 3:1–4, Solomon observes there is "a time to weep, and a time to laugh... a time to mourn, and a time to dance." Grieving is ordained by God as part of our earthly journey.
- **Distinguish Grief from Guilt.** Grief honors what was good; guilt burdens what was wrong. You may mourn the companionship even if the tie was ungodly. Give yourself permission to feel sorrow without shaming your decision to break the bond.

8.1.2 Stages of Grief in a Spiritual Context

While grief is unique to each person, several stages often emerge:

1. **Shock & Denial.** An initial numbness or disbelief—"I can't really be free from this... can I?"
2. **Pain & Guilt.** Waves of sorrow, shame, or regret arise as memories surface. You may wonder if you acted rashly.
3. **Anger & Bargaining.** You might feel anger at yourself, the other person, or God. Bargaining thoughts—"If only I'd done X..."—may tempt you to reconnect.
4. **Depression & Withdrawal.** Deep sadness can lead to isolation, as you grapple with loneliness (2 Cor 1:3–4).
5. **Acceptance & Hope.** Gradually, the fog lifts. You begin to sense God's presence and look forward to new life in Him.

Key Insight: Grieving is not linear; you may revisit stages. The Spirit's role is to guide you through each season, turning mourning into dancing (Psalm 30:11).

8.1.3 Rituals and Practices to Process Loss

God often uses tangible acts to shape our inner journey.

- **Journaling Your Lament.** Write letters you won't send—pouring out grief, questions, and even anger to God. He invites us to "pour out our hearts" before Him (Psalm 62:8).
- **Memorial Acts.** Create a small ceremony marking the end of the bond: write the other person's name on a paper, then ceremonially tear or burn it, declaring, "I release you, and I release myself from this tie." Jeremiah 23:29 affirms that God's word is like a fire that purges and refines.
- **Space for Tears.** Jesus wept openly (John 11:35). Don't suppress tears; allow them a place to fall— whether before the Lord, with a trusted friend, or in a journal. Tears are God's gift to cleanse the soul.
- **Lament Psalms.** Pray or meditate on Psalms of lament—e.g., Psalm 42, 88, or 130. These scriptures give voice to deep pain and model how to turn to God mid-sorrow.

8.2 Rebuilding Self-Worth in Christ

A severed soul tie often destabilizes our self-image. If we had anchored our value in another's affirmation or in the illusion of that bond, we must now rebuild our identity on the unshakeable foundation of Christ.

8.2.1 Understanding Your New Identity

The New Covenant declares that our true identity is found **in Christ**, not in any human connection.

- **Child of God.** "See what kind of love the Father has given to us, that we should be called children of God" (1 John 3:1). Embrace this truth daily—your worth is based on God's love, not another's approval.
- **Co-heirs with Christ.** Romans 8:17 assures us, "If indeed we suffer with him, we will also be glorified with him." Your inheritance includes dignity, purpose, and value that no human tie can match or diminish.
- **New Creation.** "Therefore, if anyone is in Christ, he is a new creation. The old has passed away; behold, the new has come" (2 Cor 5:17). Let go of past shame and step into the newness of life, viewing yourself through the lens of redemption.

8.2.2 Renewing the Mind through Scripture

Our thoughts shape our sense of worth. Renewing the mind with God's truth replaces lies with life.

- **Scripture Memorization.** Commit to memory key verses about your identity—Psalm 139:13–14 ("I am fearfully and wonderfully made"), Ephesians 2:10 ("We are his workmanship"), and Romans 12:2 ("Be transformed by the renewal of your mind").
- **Taste and See.** Meditate on one verse a day using the **SOAP** method: Scripture, Observation, Application, Prayer. This helps internalize truth and align your thinking with God's perspective.
- **Thought-Stopping Techniques.** When you catch self-degrading or bondage-driven thoughts—"I'll never be free"—immediately replace them with a truth statement: "In Christ, I am free from condemnation" (Romans 8:1). Over time, this habit rewires your thought patterns.

8.2.3 Practicing Self-Compassion and Spiritual Self-Care

Loving ourselves well is not selfish; it prepares us to love others out of fullness rather than neediness.

- **Sabbath Rest.** Honor God's command to rest (Exodus 20:8–10). Taking a day to cease labor, enjoy creation, and meet with God rejuvenates body, soul, and spirit.
- **Healthy Habits.** Exercise, adequate sleep, and balanced nutrition support emotional resilience. Your body is God's temple (1 Cor 6:19); caring for it honors Him and aids healing.
- **Creative Expression.** Engage in art, music, or poetry to process emotions. David played the lyre to soothe his soul (1 Sam 16:23); you too can use creativity as a channel for healing.
- **Gratitude Practice.** Keep a gratitude journal, listing daily blessings. Paul urges us to "give thanks in all circumstances" (1 Thess 5:18). Focusing on God's goodness counteracts the negativity of loss.

8.3 Community & Accountability

Healing in isolation is perilous. God designs us for **koinonia**— deep fellowship—so that others can bear us up (Heb 10:24–25). The right community both comforts and challenges, bearing fruit in lasting restoration.

8.3.1 Communing with the Body of Christ

- **Regular Gathering.** Commit to weekly worship services and small groups where you can receive teaching, prayer, and encouragement. Acts 2:42–47 describes the early church's devoted fellowship, a model for today.
- **Authentic Sharing.** Safe spaces—such as a women's or men's group—allow honest confession and mutual prayer. James 5:16 tells us, "Confess your sins to one another and pray for one another, that you may be healed."
- **Spiritual Gifts Deployment.** Serving in ministry shifts focus from self-healing to others' needs. 1 Peter 4:10 exhorts us to use whatever gift we have to serve, as faithful stewards. As you bless others, your own wounds receive balm.

8.3.2 Finding Safe Relationships for Accountability

Not all friendships are equally suited for this season of restoration. Choose relationships marked by integrity, wisdom, and confidentiality.

- **Mentors and Spiritual Parents.** Seek someone mature in faith who can speak truth in love (Proverbs 27:17). Regular check-ins help you stay on track, especially when old temptations or grief resurface.
- **Support Groups.** Many churches host ministry-specific groups—e.g., recovery, divorce care, sexual purity. These groups combine biblical teaching with peer support and practical steps toward freedom.
- **Boundary-Aware Friends.** Invite one or two trusted friends to partner with you. Define the scope: what you will share, how often you'll meet, and when to bring in a counselor if deeper wounds arise.

8.3.3 Professional and Pastoral Support

Sometimes wounds run too deep for lay ministry alone.

- **Counseling Referrals.** A Christian counselor can integrate psychological tools (CBT, EMDR) with spiritual care, guiding you through trauma and maladaptive patterns.
- **Pastoral Care.** Pastors and chaplains offer regular prayer, biblical counsel, and sacramental means of grace (e.g., anointing with oil, liturgical prayers) to reinforce healing.
- **Deliverance Teams.** For longstanding ties with occultic or demonic dimensions, a trained deliverance ministry can provide corporate intercession and spiritual warfare support (Luke 10:17–20).

8.4 Walking Forward in Newness

Though our outline highlights three core routes—grief, personal rebuilding, and community—true restoration weaves them together into ongoing **growth cycles**. As you grieve, you reaffirm your identity in Christ; as you rebuild self-worth, you step deeper into community; as community upholds you, you find courage to press into new seasons of service.

- **Celebrate Milestones.** Mark anniversaries of your break-off with prayer retreats or thanksgiving services. Psalm 126:3 declares, "The Lord has done great things for us; we are glad."
- **Develop New Soul Ties.** Over time, healthy bonds—friendships, mentorships, ministry partnerships—fill the space once occupied by the ungodly tie. Guard these new ties with biblical boundaries (2 Cor 6:14).
- **Maintain Spiritual Habits.** A daily rhythm of prayer, Scripture, worship, and rest prevents old patterns from re-emerging. Let your life be an altar where God's ongoing grace is both received and offered to others (Rom 12:1–2).

Chapter 9 – Building Godly Relationships Going Forward

Having broken ungodly soul ties and walked through deliverance, grief, and restoration, we now turn to the proactive work of forging **healthy, kingdom-centered bonds** that honor God and enrich our lives. In this chapter, we'll explore three foundational arenas for Godly relationships: **Biblical Friendship Ethics**, **Courtship & Dating with Discernment**, and **Marriage: Keeping the Bond Holy**. Each section offers concrete principles, practical steps, and Scriptural examples to guide you in cultivating ties that reflect Christ's love, protect your soul, and multiply grace in the world.

9.1 Biblical Friendship Ethics

Friendship, when rooted in Christ, becomes a channel of grace—spurring us toward holiness, bearing our burdens, and cheering on our faith. Yet not every connection qualifies as a "friend." Scripture gives us clear criteria for selecting, nurturing, and preserving godly friendships.

Proverbs 13:20 – "Whoever walks with the wise becomes wise, but the companion of fools will suffer harm."

- **Assess Character, Not Convenience.** Seek friends whose lives exhibit the fruit of the Spirit (Gal 5:22–23): love, joy, peace, patience, kindness, goodness, faithfulness, gentleness, self-control.
- **Shared Values Over Shared Interests.** While hobbies and cultural affinities can connect you, the deepest friendships form around common devotion to Christ (Amos 3:3: "Do two walk together unless they have agreed?").
- **Warning Signs.** If a prospective friend dismisses biblical authority, encourages compromise, or thrives on gossip, heed Solomon's warning: "Bad company ruins good morals" (1 Cor 15:33).

Practical Steps

1. **Observe before Opening Up.** Spend initial months in group settings, watching how they treat others, handle correction, and respond under stress.
2. **Ask Honest Questions.** Over coffee, discuss faith convictions: "What are your non-negotiables in your walk with God?"
3. **Set Small Tests of Trust.** Invite them to pray with you for a simple need. Their response reveals spiritual sincerity more than shared favorite movies.

9.1.2 Qualities of a Godly Friend

John 15:13 – "Greater love has no one than this, that someone lay down his life for his friends." A godly friend reflects Christ's sacrificial love in four key ways:

1. **Honesty in Love.** Proverbs 27:6 notes, "Faithful are the wounds of a friend; profuse are the kisses of an enemy." True friends speak hard truths gently, correcting false steps rather than affirming sin.

2. **Loyalty Under Trial.** Ruth's pledge to Naomi—
   "Where you go I will go" (Ruth 1:16)—models
   steadfastness. A godly friend remains even when it
   costs popularity or convenience.
3. **Encouragement in Weakness.** Barnabas, "son of
   encouragement," sought out discouraged Paul (Acts
   11:25–26). Encourage each other with Scripture: "I
   thank my God... when I remember you" (Phil 1:3).
4. **Prayerful Intercession.** "Pray for one another"
   (James 5:16). A friend who regularly lifts you before
   the throne participates in your spiritual health.

Cultivating These Qualities

- **Practice "Iron Sharpening"** (Prov 27:17): invite
  mutual feedback on prayer life, Bible study, and
  fruitfulness.
- **Establish "Safe Words."** Agree on phrases like "I
  need honesty" to signal times for loving correction.
- **Share Prayer Calendars.** List prayer requests and
  check in weekly; transparency in prayer cements
  relational trust.

9.1.3 Cultivating Mutual Encouragement

**Hebrews 10:24–25 – "Let us consider how to stir up one
another to love and good works... encouraging one
another, and all the more as you see the Day drawing
near."**

- **Celebrate Spiritual Milestones.** Baptisms, answered
  prayers, and moments of obedience deserve
  communal rejoicing (Luke 15:7).
- **Seasonal Pairings.** In busy seasons—new
  parenthood, job transitions—pair up so each bears half
  the emotional load.
- **Group Accountability.** Launch a "3×3" model: three
  friends who each meet one-on-one weekly for prayer,
  accountability on sin struggles, and goal-setting in
  ministry.

- **Encouragement Journals.** Write one encouraging note per friend each month; exchange journals quarterly to see growth.
- **Shared Scripture Memory.** Memorize verses together (e.g., Romans 8:38–39), quizzing each other to reinforce truth.
- **Celebration Rituals.** A simple "Victory Circle" at the end of small-group meetings where each person shares one victory and one prayer need.

9.1.4 Conflict Resolution and Forgiveness

Matthew 18:15–17 – "If your brother sins against you, go and tell him his fault... If he listens, you have gained your brother." Christ's method for conflict is direct, humble, and redemptive.

1. **Private Confrontation.** First approach in love and gentleness, focusing on behavior ("when you do X, I feel Y"), not character assassination.
2. **Bring Witnesses if Needed.** If private appeals fail, involve one or two mature believers to mediate—"so that every charge may be established by the evidence of two or three witnesses" (2 Cor 13:1).
3. **Restoration Over Retribution.** The aim is mutual restoration, not punishment. Paul warns: "Do not avenge yourselves... but leave room for the wrath of God" (Rom 12:19).

Forgiveness Practices

- **Prayer for the Offender.** James 5:16 links confession with prayer—pray for the one who hurt you before confronting them, softening your heart.
- **Symbolic Release.** Write the offense on paper, then shred or burn it, declaring, "Jesus has borne this, and I release it."
- **Ongoing Reconciliation.** Forgiveness requires forgetting in the sense of not replaying the offense—

"Love keeps no record of wrongs" (1 Cor 13:5). When memories surface, counter them with Scripture declarations of grace.

9.2 Courtship & Dating with Discernment

In a culture of casual romance, the biblical model of **intentional, covenant-minded courtship** stands out. Courtship—with its guided steps, accountability, and clear purpose—protects hearts from needless wounds and ensures physical, emotional, and spiritual alignment before marriage.

9.2.1 Defining Biblical Courtship

Ruth & Boaz (Ruth 2–4) and **Isaac & Rebekah (Gen 24)** offer prototypical glimpses of courtship:

- **Family and Community Involvement.** Abraham sent his servant to his homeland (Gen 24:3–4), seeking parental blessing. Boaz involved kinsmen (Ruth 4:1–12), publicizing the union.
- **Work and Waiting.** Boaz invited Ruth to glean (Ruth 2:8–9), building trust over time—no hidden agendas, only observable character.
- **Covenantal Vows.** Both stories culminate in public vows before the community, sealing the intent to marry.

Principles for Today

1. **Clarity of Intent.** Ask, "Are we seeking marriage or companionship?" If the goal is marriage, articulate it early to align expectations.
2. **Parental (& Pastoral) Blessing.** Though not mandatory, inviting wise elders honors Scripture's pattern of counsel (Prov 11:14) and adds accountability.
3. **Courtship Period.** Establish a defined season (e.g., 6–12 months) to evaluate compatibility—spiritual

vision, family values, communication styles—without undue prolongation.

9.2.2 Setting Boundaries in Dating

2 Corinthians 6:14 – "Do not be unequally yoked with unbelievers." 1 Thessalonians 4:3–5 – "For this is the will of God, your sanctification: that you abstain from sexual immorality… controlling your own body in holiness and honor."

- **Physical Boundaries.** Agree on what is and isn't permissible: public vs. private settings, no prolonged alone time in intimate spaces, no sexual activity outside marriage.
- **Emotional Boundaries.** Guard against prematurely deep emotional entanglement—avoid "love bombing" or intense declarations in early weeks; reserve vulnerable disclosures until substantial trust is built.
- **Spiritual Boundaries.** Commit to joint Bible study times and prayer before solitary conversations about sensitive topics, ensuring the Holy Spirit's presence directs your dialogue.

Boundary-Setting Practices

- **Accountability Agreement.** Share your dating boundaries with a mentor couple who will check in monthly for encouragement and course-correction.
- **Public Courtship.** Meet in groups or public venues for the first several months—cafés, church events, service projects—minimizing temptation and adding communal oversight.
- **Digital Discipline.** Avoid late-night texting or video calls. Agree on "phone curfews" (e.g., no calls after 9 pm) to prevent emotional vulnerability when self-control is low.

Amos 3:3 – "Do two walk together, unless they have agreed to meet?" Beyond chemistry, courtship demands deep alignment on four pillars:

1. **Core Doctrinal Convictions.** Attend separate denomination or doctrinal discussion groups—ensure agreement on atonement, Scripture, baptism, and mission.
2. **Life Vision & Calling.** Compare long-term goals: career aspirations, church involvement, views on children and parenting.
3. **Conflict Styles & Communication.** Take a premarital workshop to practice resolving disagreements in biblical ways (Eph 4:2–3).
4. **Financial Stewardship.** Discuss attitudes toward money, debt, generosity, and tithing habits (Prov 22:7; 2 Cor 9:7).

Tools for Evaluation

- **Pre-Marriage Inventory.** Use a biblically based questionnaire (e.g., Prepare/Enrich) with a certified counselor to surface differences and strengths.
- **Mentor Couple Feedback.** After meeting your mentor couple together, invite them to share observations on your compatibility and blind spots.
- **Trial Service Projects.** Serve together in a ministry area—missions trip, homeless outreach—observing how you collaborate, encourage each other, and deal with hardship.

9.2.4 Intentional Community Involvement

Ecclesiastes 4:9–10 – "Two are better than one... if either of them falls down, one can help the other up." Courtship flourishes in the context of the wider body:

- **Group Mentoring.** Join a "courtship circle" of engaged and married couples who meet quarterly to share experiences, pray, and offer counsel.
- **Church Accountability.** Regularly report milestones—meeting families, setting boundaries—to a pastor or small-group leader.
- **Peer Encouragement.** Pair with another courtship or engaged couple for reciprocal support, sharing prayer needs and celebrating spiritual growth.

9.3 Marriage: Keeping the Bond Holy

Marriage is the highest human bond, a covenant image of Christ and His Church (Eph 5:25–33). To build a marriage that honors God and resists ungodly soul ties, intentional spiritual and practical rhythms are essential.

9.3.1 Covenantal Foundations

Genesis 2:24 – "A man shall leave his father and his mother and hold fast to his wife, and they shall become one flesh." Malachi 2:14 – "The LORD was witness between you and the wife of your youth, to whom you have been faithless…"

- **Leaving, Cleaving, Becoming One.** "Leaving" denotes releasing primary loyalty from parents; "cleaving" (*dābaq*) speaks of sacrificial allegiance to spouse.
- **Public Covenant.** Your wedding vows are not merely legal promises but spiritual commitments "in the sight of God and these witnesses." Treat them with the gravity of Malachi's rebuke of unfaithfulness.
- **Ongoing Renewal.** Like the Israelites renewing the covenant (Josh 24:25–26), revisit your vows annually—renew them privately and in a small congregation of friends and family.

9.3.2 Cultivating Spiritual Intimacy

1 Corinthians 7:3–5 – "Do not deprive one another, except perhaps... but consenually, for a time, that you may devote yourselves to prayer." Ephesians 5:31–33 – "'...they shall become one flesh.' This mystery is profound, and I am saying that it refers to Christ and the church."

- **Couple Prayer Time.** Schedule daily—morning or evening—30 minutes alone together to pray, read Scripture, and share spiritual highlights.
- **Mutual Service Projects.** Serve side-by-side—local outreach, discipleship ministries—to cultivate teamwork under God's leading.
- **Sexual Intimacy as Covenant Expression.** Approach your physical union as spiritual worship, not as mere recreation. Discuss desires, boundaries, and mutual care (Song of Solomon; Hebrews 13:4).

Enhancing Spiritual Connection

- **Nightly "Highs & Lows."** Share one spiritual high (God's faithfulness) and one low (areas of struggle) each evening to keep communication transparent.
- **Couple's Devotional.** Use a marriage devotional book—such as Francis Chan's *You and Me Forever*—to guide weekly discussions about faith and priorities.
- **Attend Marriage Retreats.** Quarterly retreats offer expert teaching, counseling check-ins, and time away from daily pressures to refocus on each other and on Christ.

9.3.3 Seasonal Support and Conflict Management

Ecclesiastes 4:12 – "A threefold cord is not quickly broken." Ephesians 4:2–3 – "Be completely humble and gentle; be patient, bearing with one another in love, eager to maintain the unity of the Spirit in the bond of peace."

- **Recognize Seasons.** Marriage has seasons—parenting young children, career changes, empty-nest. Each requires new rhythms of support: date nights, prayer groups, childcare swaps.
- **Conflict-Resolution Blueprint.**
    1. **Cool-Down Time.** When tempers flare, agree on a signal to take space (30 minutes) before discussion.
    2. **I-Statements.** Express needs clearly: "I feel hurt when…" rather than "You always…"
    3. **Third-Party Help.** If stuck, consult a trusted mentor couple or counselor—"Without counsel plans fail, but with many advisers they succeed" (Prov 15:22).
- **Triadic Support.** Enlist a "threefold cord" of mutual friends or family who intercede for you, celebrate milestones, and model healthy marriage.

9.3.4 Nurturing Family Worship and Legacy

Deuteronomy 6:6–9 – "These words that I command you today shall be on your heart…but you shall teach them diligently to your children…" Joshua 24:15 – "As for me and my house, we will serve the LORD."

- **Daily Family Devotions.** Even if children are small, read a brief passage each morning, sing a hymn, and pray over the day ahead—instilling God's presence at home's center.
- **Weekly Family Altar.** Designate one evening for meal, Scripture reading, and collective prayers—covering neighbors, missionaries, and each family member's needs.
- **Generational Storytelling.** Share testimonies of how God delivered you from ungodly ties; these narratives become heirlooms of faith for grandchildren.
- **Hospitality as Discipleship.** Regularly host other families or young couples in your home. Practicing hospitality (1 Pet 4:9) not only blesses guests but reinforces the gospel in your household.

Chapter 10 – Special Contexts & Contemporary Challenges

In an age marked by rapid social change, technological innovation, and complex family dynamics, soul ties take on new shapes and pose fresh challenges. This chapter examines three "special contexts" in which soul ties can entangle us—**family systems and generational patterns**, **digital-age connections**, and **ministry/leadership relationships**—and offers biblically grounded wisdom for navigating each. By understanding how bonds operate in these arenas and applying kingdom principles, you can walk in freedom and foster soul ties that honor Christ even amid contemporary pressures.

10.1 Family Systems & Generational Ties

Every family functions as a system of roles, expectations, and emotional currents that shape how we bond with parents, siblings, and ancestors. These multigenerational dynamics often embed soul ties—both healthy and unhealthy—that influence our identity, decision-making, and spiritual life.

- **Generational Curses and Blessings.**
    - *Old Testament Warning*: "I, the Lord your God, am a jealous God... visiting the iniquity of the fathers on the children to the third and fourth generation" (Ex 20:5).
    - *New Covenant Hope*: "Christ redeemed us from the curse of the law by becoming a curse for us" (Gal 3:13). Through Him, curses lose their hold and blessings flow afresh.
- **Common Patterns. 1. Repeated Sin Tendencies.** Addiction, abuse, or dishonesty passed from grandparents to parents affects children's soul patterns. 2. **Emotional Legacies.** Shame, perfectionism, or people-pleasing may become family hallmarks, binding souls to unspoken demands. 3. **Spiritual Heritage.** Faith and godly values—in worship, prayer, or hospitality—can also weave generational soul ties, equipping descendants with a gospel legacy.
- **Case Study.** A third-generation alcoholic discovers early family trauma fueled the addiction pattern. Only after godly prayer and renunciation of ancestral vows (Num 30; Jer 4:14) does true freedom emerge.

10.1.2 Birth Order, Roles, and Expectations

- **Firstborns, Middlers, and Youngest Children.**
    - Firstborns may bear the burden of leadership or perfection, tying self-worth to performance.
    - "Middle children" often struggle for recognition, forging soul ties of envy or approval-seeking.
    - The youngest may develop patterns of dependence.
- **Scriptural Reflection.** Isaac favored Esau over Jacob (Gen 25:28), sowing rivalry; Rachel's longing for a child led to soul ties of envy toward Leah (Gen 29:31–35).
- **Practical Insight.** Understanding your family role clarifies why certain relational bonds feel compulsive.

A firstborn's need to please authority figures may create ungodly ties to supervisors or church leaders.

10.1.3 Breaking Generational Soul Ties

- **Step 1: Identify Patterns.** Prayerfully map family history—note recurring sins, emotional wounds, or spiritual blind spots.
- **Step 2: Corporate Confession.** In solidarity, pray: "Lord, forgive my lineage for [specific sins]. We renounce every curse and vow rooted in our family line."
- **Step 3: Claim Redemption.** Declare Galatians 3:13: "Christ has redeemed me from every generational curse."
- **Step 4: Establish New Traditions.** Replace toxic rituals with godly practices—weekly family devotion, shared service projects, or storytelling of God's faithfulness in your line.

10.1.4 Recasting Family Identity in Christ

- **Adoption into God's Family.** "But when the fullness of time had come, God sent forth his Son... for those who were led by the Spirit of God, he called sons of God" (Gal 4:4–6). Your primary soul tie is now to your heavenly Father.
- **Family Altar Practices.** Deuteronomy 6:6–7 commands teaching God's commands at home. Hosting weekly family worship breaks unhealthy generational ties and anchors new ones in Christ.
- **Mutual Accountability.** In close-knit families, establish "circle of trust" meetings to share struggles, pray, and reinforce gospel identity over ingrained familial roles (Eccl 4:9–12).

10.2 Digital-Age Soul Ties

The internet, smartphones, and social media have expanded opportunities for connection—but they also create novel soul-binding dynamics. Virtual intimacy, 24/7 accessibility, and curated online personas can forge ties as powerful as face-to-face ones, yet more subtle and harder to discern.

10.2.1 Virtual Relationships & Emotional Bonding

- **Parasocial Connections.**
    - Following influencers or podcasters can feel like two-way friendship, yet the bond is one-sided. Undue emotional investment here can divert your affection from Christ and real community.
    - *Biblical Parallel*: Israelites worshiped the golden calf, a man-made image they bonded to instead of Yahweh (Ex 32). Virtual idols likewise claim loyalty.
- **Anonymous Intimacy.**
    - Online forums allow deep sharing under pseudonyms. While cathartic, the lack of accountability can foster soul ties to strangers—especially around trauma disclosure—without spiritual oversight.
    - *Guideline*: Share vulnerable material only within trusted, vetted online communities that submit to biblical oversight and confidentiality agreements.
- **Screens as Third Party.**
    - Frequent FaceTime chats with a non-spousal friend can simulate physical intimacy, triggering oxytocin release similar to in-person contact.
    - *Practice*: Set "digital boundaries"—e.g., no video calls after 9 pm, restrict to group chats, and avoid one-on-one late-night messaging.

10.2.2 Social Media & Comparative Idolatry

- **Highlight Reel Anxiety.**
    - Comparing your behind-the-scenes life to others' curated posts fuels envy—a root of Satan's attack (John 13:27). Persistent

comparison can bind your self-worth to social-media metrics (likes, comments).

- o *Scriptural Antidote*: "Do not be conformed to this world, but be transformed by the renewal of your mind" (Rom 12:2). Regularly fast from feeds and meditate on contentment texts (Phil 4:11–13).
- **Tribalism and Echo Chambers.**
  - o Algorithms reinforce beliefs, creating online "bubbles." Soul ties to ideological groups can harden into idolatrous loyalty, eclipsing Christ's unifying call (Eph 2:14).
  - o *Counterpractice*: Intentionally follow respected Christian voices from diverse backgrounds and commit weekly to pray for someone outside your usual circle.
- **Public Persona vs. Private Self.**
  - o Maintaining a "brand" can lead to dual life—an online self that pleases followers and a private self that bears unaddressed wounds. This split fosters internal soul tension.
  - o *Remedy*: Reserve one day a week as "social-media Sabbath" (Ex 20:8–10), evaluating online disclosure in prayer and aligning actions with authentic identity in Christ.

10.2.3 Online Intimacy & Pornography

- **Digital Sexual Entanglement.**
  - o Cyberspace provides immediate access to sexual content. Each viewing deepens neurological and spiritual ties—mirroring the "one body" principle of 1 Cor 6:16.
  - o *Bible's Warning*: "Flee from sexual immorality. Every other sin a person commits is outside the body, but the sexually immoral person sins against his own body" (1 Cor 6:18).
- **Dopamine-Driven Bonding.**
  - o Pornography triggers dopamine surges, forging brain pathways that cling to the screen

as a "partner." Spiritually, these become false soul ties that rival love for Christ.
- *Freedom Steps*:
    - **Technical Barriers**: Use accountability software and device filters.
    - **Immediate Fleeing**: "Flee youthful passions" (2 Tim 2:22) by shifting focus—listen to worship music, read Scripture, or call an accountability partner.
    - **Deliverance Prayer**: Renounce ties in Jesus' name and invite the Spirit's cleansing (Ps 51:10).
- **Online "Affairs" and Emotional Adultery.**
    - Intimate texting or image-sharing creates emotional bonds that, though "only words," constitute spiritual adultery (Matt 5:28).
    - *Wise Practices*:
        - Avoid private networks with romantic potential.
        - Keep all cross-gender conversations group-based or transparent.
        - Enlist a mentor to review your cyber-boundaries monthly.

10.2.4 Digital Fast & Media Boundaries

- **Rhythms of Rest.**
    - Jesus modeled withdrawal (Mark 1:35). Periodic digital fasts—24-hour or weekend sabbaths—break unhealthy ties and cultivate presence with God and others.
    - *Implementation*: Schedule one full day per month offline; replace screen time with nature walks, journaling, or face-to-face fellowship.
- **Content Diet.**
    - Curate your feed: unfollow accounts that trigger comparison, sexual temptation, or anxiety. Follow those promoting gospel truth, beauty, and goodness (Phil 4:8).

- Group Accountability: In small groups, share your "curation report" quarterly—what you removed, why, and how it impacted your soul.
- **Guarding the Heart.**
  - "Above all else, guard your heart, for everything you do flows from it" (Prov 4:23). Treat media like a saboteur seeking to breach your soul's defenses.
  - Practical Tip: Before tapping into any platform, pause and pray: "Lord, guide my eyes and heart. Protect me from ungodly soul ties." Ninety-second pauses can interrupt compulsive scrolling.

10.3 Ministry & Leadership Pitfalls

For those in pastoral, teaching, or lay-leadership roles, relationships carry additional spiritual weight. Congregants, mentees, and peers may forge soul ties with you—sometimes healthy, other times burdensome or abusive. Navigating these dynamics requires humility, accountability, and clear boundaries.

10.3.1 Codependent Pastoral Bonds

- **The "Rescuer" Problem.**
  1. Leaders who constantly "fix" others risk being emotionally enmeshed: congregants defer to them for every decision, creating a soul tie that worships the leader rather than God.
  2. Biblical Example: Moses, overwhelmed by judging disputes, needed Jethro's counsel to delegate (Ex 18:13–27). Leaders who fail to delegate invite unhealthy bonds.
- **Boundary Solutions.**
  1. **Role Clarity**: Define pastoral scope—spiritual guidance, not financial or familial rescue.
  2. **Scheduled Availability**: Office hours or appointment systems prevent 24/7 dependency.

3. **Team-Based Care**: Share counseling duties among qualified staff or lay counselors to distribute emotional load.

10.3.2 Celebrity Christian Culture

- **Elevation and Idolatry.**
    - High-profile pastors or speakers can become "icons," attracting fan-like soul ties that resemble celebrity worship more than biblical discipleship.
    - *Paul's Caution*: "I pleasure to preach the gospel... lest the cross of Christ be emptied of its power" (1 Cor 9:16–17). When platform eclipses message, souls become bound to personalities.
- **Countermeasures.**
    - **Substance Over Style**: Evaluate teaching by Scriptural depth, not production value.
    - **Personal Discipleship**: Prioritize local church relationships where leaders live among congregants, preventing distance-fueled idolization.
    - **Transparency and Vulnerability**: Leaders who share testimonies of weakness counteract the myth of infallibility, redirecting soul ties to Christ's sufficiency (2 Cor 12:9–10).

10.3.3 Power Dynamics & Spiritual Abuse

- **Misuse of Authority.**
    1. Leaders may demand loyalty, withhold grace, or manipulate membership—creating coercive soul ties that hinder freedom (Matt 23:4).
    2. *Case in Point*: The letters to the seven churches in Revelation critique overbearing, loveless, or complacent leadership (Rev 2–3).
- **Safeguarding Structures.**
    1. **Accountability Boards**: Pastors answer to a council of peers or elders, ensuring checks on power.

2. **Clear Complaint Processes**: Confidential channels for congregants to report abuses without fear of reprisal (James 5:14).
3. **Regular Leadership Evaluations**: Annual outside reviews—both spiritual and professional—foster humility and renewal.

10.3.4 Healthy Leader-Congregant Soul Ties

- **Mutual Submission in Love.**
    - Ephesians 5:21 calls us to "submit to one another out of reverence for Christ." Leaders "shepherd the flock" (1 Pet 5:2–3) as servants, not lords.
    - *Practical Rhythm*: Incorporate "leader day" events where ministers receive care—prayer, rest, honest feedback—so their soul ties with congregants remain life-giving.
- **Mentorship Over Dependency.**
    - Encourage congregants to seek spiritual guidance from multiple mentors, not idolize a single pastor.
    - *Discipleship Networks*: Equip lay leaders ("disciples of disciples") so care multiplies beyond pastoral office, preventing bottlenecks of dependence.

Chapter 11 – Case Studies & Testimonies

Real-life stories breathe life into doctrine, illustrating how soul ties form, ensnare, and—even more powerfully—how Christ's freedom breaks their hold. In this chapter, you'll encounter **personal narratives** of believers who walked from bondage into newness, **pastoral counseling vignettes** showing ministry in action, and then a careful **analytical commentary** highlighting patterns, pitfalls, and keys to lasting redemption. As you meditate on these cases, may the Lord encourage you that no tie is too strong for His grace.

11.1 Personal Narratives of Freedom

11.1.1 Sarah's Journey from Codependency to Christ-Centered Identity

Sarah grew up in a home where approval was scarce. As the eldest daughter, she learned early that affection came only when she excelled—straight A's, perfect church attendance, unceasing service to her younger siblings. By her mid-20s,

Sarah's identity was bound to performance and the approval of a controlling boyfriend, Tom.

- **Formation of the Tie.** Tom showered her with praise when she met his expectations—cooking, cleaning, and centering weekend plans on his whims. Every time she "failed" (missed a call, spoke her own mind), he withdrew affection. Soon Sarah found herself compulsively checking her phone, anxious over his late replies.
    1. *Bible Reference:* "Whatever you do, work heartily, as for the Lord and not for men" (Col 3:23) warns against human-approval–driven service.
- **Signs of Bondage.** Sarah's daily rhythms revolved around anticipating Tom's demands. She canceled nursing-study sessions to visit him, skipped small-group prayer to care for his emotional turmoil, and felt guilty if she chose personal rest.
- **Breaking Point.** When Tom's anger turned to threats, Sarah realized the tie had become toxic. In tearful prayer, she confessed her codependency (1 John 1:9) and renounced every vow she'd made to earn his love (Jer 4:14).
- **Path to Restoration.**
    1. **Repentance & Renunciation:** With her pastor, she prayed a renunciation prayer: "I revoke every promise that said, 'I will earn affection by performance.'"
    2. **Deliverance & Inner Healing:** In weekly sessions, Sarah processed childhood wounds—her father's emotional neglect—and replaced lies ("I must perform to be loved") with truths from Psalm 139 ("I am fearfully and wonderfully made").
    3. **Boundary-Setting:** She blocked Tom's number, declined visits, and established phone-curfews—no calls after 8 pm—protecting her mind and heart (Prov 4:23).

4. **Rebuilding Identity:** Memorizing Galatians 2:20 and journaling daily, she declared, "It is no longer I who live, but Christ who lives in me."
5. **New Soul Ties:** Sarah joined a women's discipleship group, cultivating friendships rooted in mutual vulnerability and prayer (Eccl 4:9–10).

Over six months, anxiety attacks subsided, compulsive texting ceased, and Sarah felt the "old self" loosen its grip. Today she works as a nurse, thriving in healthy friendships and anchored in Christ's unconditional love.

11.1.2 Mark's Breakthrough from Pornography Soul Tie

Mark, a 32-year-old software engineer, first encountered pornography in college. What began as curiosity quickly became habit. Late-night surfing released a rush that seemed to soothe social anxiety and loneliness. Each session deepened a neurological bond, embedding pornography as his "go-to" emotional comfort.

- **Formation of the Tie.** The pattern followed a predictable loop: stress ➔ porn use ➔ temporary relief ➔ guilt ➔ renewed stress. Scripture warns, "Flee from sexual immorality" (1 Cor 6:18), yet Mark felt powerless.
- **Entrenchment.** Over years, he hid the habit from girlfriends and even church mentors. Secretive behavior birthed shame, prompting deeper hiding—an ungodly soul tie with images on his screen.
- **Catalyst for Change.** After a roommate discovered his hidden browser history, Mark faced the humiliation of exposure. In fear and shame, he cried out, "God, I can't do this on my own."
- **Deliverance Process.**
  1. **Repentance & Renunciation:** In prayer, Mark confessed his sin (Psalm 51:1–4) and renounced the grip of porn: "I reject every image and every habitual thought that claimed authority over me."

2. **Technical and Spiritual Barriers:** He installed accountability software, appointed two accountability partners from his church, and committed to phone-free bedrooms (Matt 5:29).
3. **Inner Healing:** Through a Christian counselor, he uncovered childhood neglect—porn had served as surrogate affection. He learned to process loneliness in prayer rather than pixels.
4. **Replacing the Tie:** Each time temptation struck, Mark recited Philippians 4:8, then texted an accountability friend. He also memorized Psalm 119:9 ("How can a young man keep his way pure? By guarding it according to your word!").
5. **Community Support:** He joined a men's recovery group that met weekly for worship, teaching, and mutual confession (James 5:16).

After a year of consistent effort, Mark celebrated his one-year "clean" milestone in front of his small group—testifying that the "desire" had lost its power and the "old man" was crucified with Christ (Rom 6:6).

11.1.3 Maria's Liberation from Generational Patterns

Maria's family bore a legacy of anger and emotional abuse. Every parent–child argument escalated to shouting; every marital conflict finalized with slamming doors. Maria found herself reacting with rage at minor slights, replicating her mother's pattern.

- **Inherited Soul Tie.** From childhood, Maria's soul had been tied to her family's emotional volatility. Scripture's warning about generational iniquity (Ex 34:7) echoed in her life.
- **Signs of the Tie.** A traffic jam could trigger disproportionate anger; critique from a friend would send her into rage–apology cycles that felt uncontrollable.

- **Awakening.** After unintentionally shouting at her four-year-old son, Maria wept: "I have become my mother." Recognizing the soul tie, she sought God's help.
- **Steps to Freedom.**
  1. **Generational Renunciation:** In a family prayer meeting, Maria led a renunciation: "We break every vow of anger, distress, and humiliation sworn by our ancestors."
  2. **Redemptive Memory Work:** With a therapist, she journaled childhood snapshots, lamented them to God (Psalm 10:14), and released them symbolically—writing each memory on cards and burning them in prayer.
  3. **New Family Practices:** Maria and her husband instituted "peace circles" each evening—family devotions where everyone shares one good and one hard thing about the day, modeling calm listening.
  4. **Ongoing Accountability:** She met monthly with an elder couple who had walked similar paths, sharing victories and setbacks (Heb 10:24–25).
  5. **Affirming Truth:** Daily affirmations from Proverbs 14:29 ("Whoever is slow to anger has great understanding, but he who has a hasty temper exalts folly") rewired her thought patterns.

Within a year, Maria noticed her reactions shifting from explosive to measured. Her marriage improved, her children thrived in calm security, and Maria experienced the truth of Galatians 5:22's "fruit of the Spirit: gentleness, self-control" blossoming in her heart.

11.2 Pastoral Counseling Vignettes

11.2.1 The Thompsons' Marriage Restoration

Pastor Lee received the Thompsons, who had confessed multiple soul ties: Mrs. Thompson's codependency on her mentor, Pastor John; and Mr. Thompson's pornography habit—both causing marital estrangement.

- **Initial Assessment.** In separate sessions, the couple disclosed emotional and physical boundaries had eroded: Mrs. Thompson attended private therapy with Pastor John, gifting him special prayers; Mr. Thompson hid his phone and sneaked late-night browsing.
- **Counseling Strategy.**
  1. **Joint Repentance Service:** The church hosted a special service where the Thompsons publicly confessed their sins, naming specific ties and renouncing them (Acts 19:18–19 model).
  2. **Couple's Discipleship Plan:** Weekly marriage-focused Bible study on Ephesians 5–6, emphasizing submission, love, and spiritual warfare together.
  3. **Individual Mentorship:** Pastor Lee met with Mrs. Thompson weekly to discern healthy boundaries with male mentors and to encourage friendships with godly women. Mr. Thompson joined the church's men's purity group.
  4. **Rebuilding Trust Rituals:** The couple set aside one evening per week for "Truth & Trust"—sharing prayer requests and prayer answers, reinforcing transparency.
- **Outcome.** Within six months, Mrs. Thompson ended private mentorships and participated in women's discipleship circles; Mr. Thompson marked his phone "accountability required" and reported monthly to the elder board. Their marriage not only survived but deepened, reflecting Ephesians 4:2's "bearing with one another in love."

11.2.2 Deliverance Session with "Mark & Lisa"

Mark and Lisa came to the church's deliverance ministry, bound by overlapping soul ties: an occultic vow made unwittingly at a college Halloween ritual, and a vow of loyalty to each other that became an idol.

- **Case Details.** In college, the couple joined a "pagan ring" for thrills—reciting oaths in a dimly lit circle. Later, they repented but felt a lingering spiritual heaviness when together.
- **Ministry Approach.**
    1. **Gathering the Team:** Three trained prayer ministers joined in Luke 10:19–20 authority prayers.
    2. **Step-By-Step Dissection:** They narrated the ritual, pinpointing each spoken oath. The team led a renunciation over each vow ("We revoke this vow in Jesus' name").
    3. **Binding & Loosing:** They bound the spirits connected to the ritual—fear, control, occultic fascination—and loosed the Spirit's gifts—wisdom, love, faith (Matt 16:19).
    4. **Inner-Healing Dialogue:** Lisa wept as she forgave herself; Mark heard the Spirit say, "Child, you are mine."
- **Results.** Following the session, the couple reported the heaviness lift. They could pray together without tears blocking their voice and felt new freedom in worship (Isa 61:3's "beauty for ashes"). Over the next months, they served as deliverance prayer partners for others, testifying to the power of renunciation.

11.2.3 Small-Group Intervention in Workplace Addiction

A bi-vocational pastor, Emmanuel, observed that four men in his Sunday morning small group struggled with second-job addictions—overworking to please bosses or spouses. Their identity was tied to productivity, a modern soul tie.

- **Intervention Steps.**
    1. **Pulpit Preaching:** Emmanuel preached on Sabbath rest (Ex 20:8–11), provoking self-examination.

2. **Group Covenant:** The small group created a "Rest Covenant," pledging one tech-free sabbath day per week; making a shared "Accountability Spreadsheet" tracking rest hours.
3. **Personal Coaching:** Each man received one-on-one coaching: identifying fears ("If I don't overwork, I'm not valuable") and replacing them with truths from Matthew 11:28–30 ("Come to me, all who labor... and I will give you rest").
4. **Family Inclusion:** Husbands invited wives to observe a "rest Sabbath" together, creating new family ties centered on worship, board games, and communal meal prep.

- **Transformation.** Within three months, absenteeism decreased, marital tensions eased, and group morale soared. Members testified that shifting their "worth from workload to worship" aligned their souls to God's rhythm rather than the world's.

11.3 Analytical Commentary on Each Story

These case studies reveal several **recurring themes**, **barriers**, and **keys** for sustainable freedom.

11.3.1 Patterns Observed

1. **Hidden Formation.** Soul ties often form quietly—in childhood patterns, secret rituals, or isolated habits—escaping detection until their consequences become painful.
2. **Compounding Mechanisms.** Sin patterns (porn, codependency) combine with spiritual rights (vows, curses), creating multi-layered bondage requiring both repentance and renunciation.
3. **Community's Role.** Every breakthrough involved others: pastors, deliverance teams, small-group members. Isolation perpetuates ties; connection facilitates healing.

4. **Ritual and Symbol.** Symbolic acts—writing and burning names, formal renunciation prayers, family covenants—help internalize spiritual realities and shift soul allegiances.

11.3.2 Common Barriers to Freedom

1. **Shame and Secrecy.** Hiding sin fosters spiritual strongholds—"the one who conceals his transgressions will not prosper" (Prov 28:13).
2. **Performance-Driven Identity.** When worth is tied to achievements or relationships, guilt and relapse intensify.
3. **Lack of Spiritual Authority.** Failure to exercise "binding and loosing" under Christ's name leaves demonic footholds intact (Matt 16:19).
4. **Insufficient Boundaries.** Without clear limits, ties re-establish themselves—unmonitored communication, unguarded media use, unconfessed vows.

11.3.3 Keys to Sustainable Redemption

1. **Complete Repentance & Renunciation.** Naming every vow, curse, or pattern and explicitly renouncing it ensures no hidden legal grounds remain.
2. **Embodied Rituals.** Physical actions—burning papers, blocking numbers, Sabbath rest—align body and spirit to new allegiances.
3. **Truth-Centered Thought Replacement.** Memorizing and declaring Scripture interrupts old neural pathways and installs God's truth at lie-trigger points.
4. **Ongoing Community Accountability.** Regular check-ins, submission to mentors, and communal prayer reinforce the new soul ties of grace.
5. **Cultivation of Primary Union with Christ.** Each case re-grounded in union with Jesus (1 Cor 6:17) as the ultimate soul connection that surpasses every human bond.

Chapter 12 – Tools, Prayers & Further Resources

In the journey from bondage to freedom, practical tools and spiritual disciplines are indispensable companions. This final chapter offers a **toolkit** you can personalize: guided prayer templates to invite God's power, journaling prompts that excavate hidden ties, curated recommendations for deeper study and ministry support, and a ready-to-use small-group discussion guide. Each section is crafted to equip you for sustained breakthrough—so that freedom in Christ becomes not only a one-time deliverance but a lifestyle of flourishing soul ties.

12.1 Guided Prayer Templates

Prayer is the lifeline of the soul, the medium through which we access God's authority, grace, and healing. Below are **four** templated prayers, each targeting a key phase of the soul-tie journey. Feel free to adapt wording, insert personal names or situations, and pray aloud—your spoken faith activates God's promises (Mark 11:24).

12.1.1 Prayer for Discernment

> **Scripture Basis:** "O Lord, I know that the way of man is not in himself, that it is not in man who walks to direct his steps." (Jeremiah 10:23)
> **Purpose:** Invite the Holy Spirit to illuminate hidden bonds and patterns in your life.

Heavenly Father, I come before You in humility, acknowledging that my heart can be clouded by sin and by ties I do not fully recognize. I ask You, Spirit of Truth (John 16:13), to shine Your light into every corner of my soul. Reveal to me any relationships—past or present—that have formed unhealthy attachments. Show me patterns of codependency, vows, or hidden agreements that bind me. Grant me spiritual eyes to discern the origins of these bonds and the courage to confront them. As You have promised, "The light shines in the darkness" (John 1:5)—let that light expose every hidden knot, so that I may walk in liberty. In Jesus' name I pray. Amen.

12.1.2 Prayer for Breaking Soul Ties

> **Scripture Basis:** "It is for freedom that Christ has set us free; stand firm therefore, and do not submit again to a yoke of slavery." (Galatians 5:1)
> **Purpose:** Invoke Christ's authority to renounce and sever ungodly soul ties.

Lord Jesus, You bore our sins and broke every chain at the cross (Colossians 2:14–15). Today, I stand on Your finished work. I renounce every soul tie that is not of You—ties formed through sin, manipulation, or deception. In Your name, I revoke every vow, oath, and pledge that granted the enemy access to my heart. I command every demonic foothold to be uprooted from my life (Ephesians 6:12–13). I declare that I am no longer bound by these past connections; I am set free to serve in the newness of the Spirit (Romans 7:6). Fill me now with Your Holy Spirit, sealing me for all eternity and empowering me to walk in truth. Amen.

12.1.3 Prayer for Healing Wounds

> **Scripture Basis:** "He heals the brokenhearted and binds up their wounds." (Psalm 147:3)
> **Purpose:** Invite God's restorative touch on emotional and spiritual scars left by severed ties.

Compassionate Father, You see every tear I have shed and know every place where my heart is fractured. In Your lovingkindness, draw near to me (Psalm 34:18). I surrender these wounds to You—pain from betrayal, grief over loss, shame from sin. By Your grace, heal the inner parts of my soul (Psalm 51:10). Fill the void these injuries have left with Your perfect love (1 John 4:18). Teach me to receive Your comfort and to extend that same mercy to myself. Restore in me the joy of Your salvation (Psalm 51:12) and renew a steadfast spirit within me. I trust in You, O God, my Healer. Amen.

12.1.4 Prayer for Cultivating New Godly Bonds

> **Scripture Basis:** "Iron sharpens iron, and one man sharpens another." (Proverbs 27:17)
> **Purpose:** Invite God to orchestrate healthy, Christ-centered relationships that spur growth and accountability.

Sovereign Lord, Thank You for giving us each other as gifts to reflect Your image (Genesis 1:27) and to encourage one another in love (Hebrews 10:24–25). Lead me by Your Spirit to friendships and mentors who will sharpen me, hold me accountable, and point me to Christ. Let our connections be marked by honesty, grace, and sacrificial love (John 15:13). Help me to offer the same: to listen well, to pray faithfully, and to speak truth in love (Ephesians 4:15). May every bond I form glorify You and reflect the unity for which Jesus prayed (John 17:21). In His name I ask it. Amen.

12.2 Journaling Prompts for Self-Examination

Journaling translates fluid thoughts into tangible artifacts, exposing patterns and charting progress. Below are **four sets** of prompts—use them weekly or as needed to map your journey out of bondage and into freedom.

12.2.1 Identifying Hidden Ties

1. **Memory Trace:** List five relationships from your past that stir strong emotions—positive or negative. Describe the context and your role in each.
2. **Emotional Echo:** For each relationship, note recurring thoughts or triggers. Do certain names, dates, or locations still provoke anxiety, longing, guilt, or shame?
3. **Spiritual Rights:** Ask yourself: Did I make any promises, vows, or pledges in these relationships (spoken or unspoken)? Write them down.
4. **Scriptural Contrast:** For each promise or pledge, find a Bible verse that directly contradicts ungodly allegiance (e.g., "No longer do I call you slaves…" Gal 4:7). Reflect on how that verse speaks liberty.

12.2.2 Mapping Emotional Triggers

1. **Trigger Log:** Over one week, record every instance of emotional disturbance—jealousy, anger, sadness—identifying the stimulus (a text, a memory, a person's name).
2. **Pattern Analysis:** At week's end, cluster your log entries by theme: Are most triggers tied to loss, rejection, performance pressure?
3. **Root Exploration:** For each theme, ask: "When did I first experience this feeling?" Trace it back to your earliest memory and write a brief narrative.
4. **Prayer Response:** For each narrative, write a short prayer asking God to heal that wound, referencing Psalm 147:3 and 2 Corinthians 1:3–4.

12.2.3 Recording Deliverance Progress

1. **Deliverance Journal Header:** Create sections labeled "Repentance," "Renunciation," "Deliverance," and "Healing."
2. **Entry Checklist:** After each deliverance prayer or counseling session, jot down:
   - Date and prayer focus
   - Scriptures used
   - Emotional/spiritual sensations (peace, grief, heaviness lifting)
   - Any auditory or visual impressions from the Spirit
3. **Weekly Review:** Every Sunday, read your entries, marking the **freedom milestones**—moments when temptation's power lessened or shame subsided. Celebrate these.
4. **Adjustment Notes:** Where bondage persists, note alternative strategies: stronger boundaries, additional counseling, or follow-up prayers.

12.2.4 Celebrations of Freedom

1. **Milestone Reflections:** Write a reflection on each "clean date" (30, 60, 90 days free from a specific sin or tie), describing changes in thoughts, behaviors, and spiritual life.
2. **Gratitude List:** For every month of sustained freedom, list ten things you're grateful for—new friendships, restored sleep, joy in prayer.
3. **Letters of Encouragement:** Compose letters (that you may or may not send) to friends or mentors who supported you, thanking them and affirming how God used them in your breakthrough (Philippians 1:3).
4. **Vision Mapping:** With each milestone, revisit your purpose and calling. Write how freedom in Christ positions you to serve others more effectively (Romans 8:28–29).

12.3 Recommended Reading & Ministries

Growth thrives on solid resources. Below are **four** curated lists: timeless theology, contemporary breakthroughs, ministry partners, and specialized counseling centers.

12.3.1 Classic Theological Works

1. ***The Mortification of Sin* by John Owen**
   - A deep dive into the believer's ongoing battle with indwelling sin and practical steps to put it to death—foundational for understanding spiritual warfare in soul-ties.
2. ***Celebration of Discipline* by Richard J. Foster**
   - Explores inward and outward disciplines—including confession, meditation, simplicity—that complement the deliverance and restoration processes.
3. ***Knowing God* by J.I. Packer**
   - Anchors identity in a profound knowledge of God's character, countering identity distortions from unhealthy attachments.
4. ***Spiritual Disciplines for the Christian Life* by Donald S. Whitney**
   - A practical guide to cultivating habits—scripture memory, journaling, solitude—that reinforce freedom and guard against old ties.

12.3.2 Contemporary Books on Boundaries, Deliverance, and Healing

1. ***Boundaries: When to Say Yes, How to Say No* by Dr. Henry Cloud & Dr. John Townsend**
   - Equips you to set and maintain healthy limits in every type of relationship—essential for breaking and preventing soul-ties.
2. ***Safe Places: Experiencing God's Freedom for Emotional Healing* by Gary Oliver**

- o Offers inner-healing strategies and testimonies that parallel the deliverance models in this book.
3. ***The Bondage Breaker*** by Dr. Neil T. Anderson
   - o Presents a step-by-step approach to spiritual freedom, including identity in Christ, authority over demons, and maintaining victory.
4. ***Emotionally Healthy Spirituality*** by Peter Scazzero
   - o Integrates emotional maturity with spiritual growth, highlighting how unresolved pain impedes intimacy with God and others.

12.3.3 Reputable Ministries and Online Resources

1. **Freedom in Christ Ministries** (www.ficm.org)
   - o Offers discipleship courses and one-on-one coaching centered on living in the freedom Christ provides.
2. **Equip.org** (Christian Research Institute)
   - o Provides articles and seminars on biblical counseling, spiritual warfare, and doctrinal clarity—helpful for pastors and lay leaders.
3. **Healing Rooms Ministries International** (www.healingrooms.org)
   - o Directory of local healing rooms where believers can receive prayer, inner-healing ministry, and deliverance support.
4. **Ministry to the Forgotten and Fallen** (www.mtff.org)
   - o Focuses on deliverance, restoration, and mentoring for those caught in occultic bonds or deep trauma.

12.3.4 Counseling and Retreat Centers

1. **Bethesda Christian Counseling** (www.bethesdacounseling.org)
   - o Integrates faith and clinical psychology, specializing in trauma, abuse, and addiction recovery.
2. **Cairnwood Retreat House** (cairnwoodretreat.com)

- Spiritual retreat center offering silence, guided prayer, and group workshops on inner-healing and soul care.
3. **Pastoral Care Institute** (www.pastoralcare.org)
   - Trains pastors in counseling skills and offers client referrals for in-depth marital, family, and individual therapy.
4. **Maranatha Retreats** (www.maranatharetreats.com)
   - Hosts weekend getaways focused on spiritual renewal, worship, and small-group processing of emotional wounds.

12.4 Small-Group Discussion Guide

Small groups provide the relational context for applying what you've learned. This **five-week guide** offers discussion questions, activities, and facilitator tips to walk a cohort through discovery, deliverance, and development of healthy soul ties.

12.4.1 Week 1: Understanding Soul Ties

- **Opening Activity (15 min):**
  - Icebreaker: "Two Truths and a Tie"—each member shares two true facts and one statement about a past bond (positive or negative). Others guess which is the bond.
- **Teaching Segment (20 min):**
  - Brief recap of Chapter 1 and 2 key concepts: definitions, theological foundations, covenant language.
- **Discussion Questions (25 min):**
  - How do you understand the difference between godly and ungodly soul ties?
  - Which biblical example (David & Jonathan or Ruth & Naomi) resonates with you, and why?
- **Prayer Focus (10 min):**
  - Group prayer for spiritual eyes to see hidden ties (using Prayer 12.1.1).

12.4.2 Week 2: Identifying Personal Ties

- **Opening Activity (15 min):**
  - Journaling Prompt 12.2.1: Spend 10 minutes mapping three relationships that still stir strong emotions.
- **Sharing and Listening (20 min):**
  - In pairs, share one mapped relationship and listen without judgment.
- **Discussion Questions (25 min):**
  - What patterns emerged in your journaling about hidden ties?
  - How did mapping vows or promises help clarify the bond's nature?
- **Prayer Focus (10 min):**
  - Pray renunciation over one identified tie (using Prayer 12.1.2).

12.4.3 Week 3: Prayer and Deliverance

- **Opening Activity (10 min):**
  - Group reads aloud The Four-Step Deliverance Prayer model (p. 236–237).
- **Practice Session (30 min):**
  - In triads, take turns praying deliverance prayers over one identified issue—others observe and support.
- **Discussion Questions (15 min):**
  - What was your experience of binding and loosing?
  - How did you sense God's presence or resistance?
- **Prayer Focus (5 min):**
  - Corporate prayer commissioning each triad to continue deliverance steps in the coming week.

12.4.4 Week 4: Healing and Restoration

- **Opening Activity (10 min):**

- o Read Psalm 147:3 and share one sentence about how it speaks to your current healing need.
- **Interactive Exercise (30 min):**
  - o Journaling Prompt 12.2.2: Map emotional triggers and trace to earliest memories. Then, in pairs, pray Psalm 62:8 over those memories.
- **Discussion Questions (15 min):**
  - o How did memorial acts (journaling, symbolic burning) aid your grieving process?
  - o What new self-care rhythms have you adopted for rebuilding worth?
- **Prayer Focus (5 min):**
  - o Group prayer for ongoing healing and restoration (using Prayer 12.1.3).

12.4.5 Week 5: Building Godly Relationships

- **Opening Activity (10 min):**
  - o Each member names one godly friend or mentor who sharpened them and shares a brief example.
- **Discussion and Planning (30 min):**
  - o Using Chapter 9's Friendship Ethics, in small teams draft a personal "friendship covenant" outlining qualities you seek and commit to embody.
- **Discussion Questions (15 min):**
  - o What boundaries will you establish to protect new bonds?
  - o How will you practice mutual encouragement in the months ahead?
- **Prayer Focus (5 min):**
  - o Closing prayer invoking God to weave new, flourishing soul ties (using Prayer 12.1.4).

12.4.6 Facilitator's Tips and Confidentiality Guidelines

1. **Establish Safe Space:** Before Week 1, have everyone sign a "Confidentiality Covenant"—what's shared in group stays in group.

2. **Time Management:** Stick to scheduled times—use a timer for discussions to ensure fairness.
3. **Emotional Check-Ins:** Begin each session with a quick emotional thermometer: rate your current state 1–10, then pray accordingly.
4. **Resource Accessibility:** Provide handouts of the prayer templates and journaling prompts. Encourage group members to enter readings or counseling contacts into their calendars.
5. **Follow-Up Plan:** After Week 5, plan a reunion at three and six months to celebrate progress, share testimonies, and re-evaluate remaining ties.

www.ingramcontent.com/pod-product-compliance
Lightning Source LLC
Chambersburg PA
CBHW060334050426
42449CB00011B/2754